sowing & reaping pizzas

sowing & reaping
pizzas

& other stories of God's unexpected faithfulness

benjamin eggers

VMI PUBLISHERS

Partnering With Christian Authors, Publishing Christian and Inspirational Books

Sisters, OR

Unless Otherwise indicated, Bible quotations are taken from New International or
Message versions of the Bible. NIV Copyright © 1973, 1978, 1984 by The International
Bible Society. Scripture taken from The Message Copyright © 1993, 1994, 1995, 1996,
2000, 2001. 2002. Used by permission of NavPress Publishing Group.

The Lion, the Witch and the Wardrobe by C. S. Lewis Copyright
© C. S. Lewis Pte. Ltd. 1950. Extract reprinted by permission
Lyrics from "Caleb's Song" Copyright © 2002 by Benjamin Eggers.
All rights reserved. Used by permission.
Lyrics from "Another Day" Copyright © 2005 by Benjamin Eggers.
All rights reserved. Used by permission.
"The Road Less Traveled" by Robert Frost (1916) This poem is in the public domain.

Published by
VMI PUBLISHERS
Sisters, Oregon
www.vmipublishers.com

ISBN: 978-1-933204-37-6

Library of Congress Control Number: 2007925387

Author Contact: www.beneggers.com

Printed in the United States of America

Cover design by Thinkbox Creative, www.thinkboxcreative.com

For Pam

My partner in faith.
Without you I would not have the courage to try,
the heart to continue, or the strength to finish.

Contents

I'm the Man?

I came into the world with a rather inauspicious beginning. My mother left me on the front steps of an orphanage in a basket of turnips. Actually, I really don't know what type of basket I was in, or if, in fact there were any turnips whatsoever, but those missing details didn't really make me feel any better about my circumstances. There is something about being dumped on the street like garbage that tends to negatively affect your ego. Go figure.

I have pictured the night many times in my mind as my mother, barely out of adolescence, stumbles through the crowded streets of Seoul, Korea with tears running down her face. (Of course it is nighttime—these things always happen after the sun has set.) She battles her self-recriminations and wishes that she were stronger. She wishes there was some other way.

She holds the bundle in her trembling arms and hopes that this one brave act will ensure a better life for this small piece of her that she gives away. She pictures the family that will take in her child. She imagines them holding and loving him—giving him everything that he needs to succeed and be happy in life. It is only because of this fragile hope that she is able to stumble on.

Finally she sees her destination. It is such a small, drab building for all the hopes and promises that she expects to be fulfilled

9

within. She glances around furtively wishing that she was invisible so that no one would witness this great act of betrayal. Knowing that her window of strength is closing fast, she steels herself and sets the basket down with only a note to tell the workers the name she has chosen to give the baby. Then she walks away. The tears on her face trailing two silver streams of regret as she forces herself onward. She doesn't look back, knowing if she did, her bravery would give way to her guilt and undo the good that she intends.

At least that's how I have always imagined it. For all I know, she could have come skipping down the street in pigtails, set me down for a moment on some steps, and gotten interested in an especially pretty butterfly and forgotten about me. (Of course, why there would be a butterfly in the middle of winter is a mystery only God will be able to solve.) You take your pick between the stories. I suppose in the end, it doesn't really matter.

So, this is the beginning of my story. Since then I have learned a bit more about the situation in Korea, and I understand that for the most part, my mother chose what was best for me. It was out of concern for me—and not some narcissistic tendency—that she gave me up for adoption. There is no welfare system in Korea and abortion is illegal, so the only choices that a young girl has if she becomes pregnant is to marry the father or offer the child up for adoption. I understand why she did it. But of course, knowing why still does not change the feelings that accompany the act.

I'm not sure if it is because of that strange beginning, or because of one of the multitude of other things that messed me up as a child, but I have a fear. It is irrational, based in insecurity, and more than a little neurotic. I am afraid of revealing too much about myself. I know it doesn't sound that bad, because many of us have that same base fear, but that's just the surface fear, the result of the root. My real fear is that if you find out too much about me, you'll just put the book down and walk away— just another mark in my litany of rejections. There, I've said it and you are still reading. My fear, baseless, as so many of them are.

I am an ordinary guy. Kind of. Two loving parents adopted me at the age of 18 months. My mother, in one of her more honest moments said that had she known how difficult it would have been to have an instant toddler, she probably wouldn't have done it. I have to say that this wasn't a statement that helped my positive self-image. But let's be honest. I have two children, and I remember what they were like as toddlers, the dirty diapers, getting into everything that they weren't supposed to, the boundless energy when all you wanted to do is sleep—aaahhh, fond memories. I remember every moment of the exquisite agony, so the fact that my mom, on her first venture into motherhood, chose to willingly subject herself to an instant toddler makes me seriously consider nominating her for sainthood.

My father was a pastor of a small church, and for my first few years in this country, we lived in Missouri. Our house was on five acres and we had a quarter horse. It was a rocky, tree-infested area with a stream and more boulders than you knew existed in the northern hemisphere. There were snakes and frogs and all sorts of things to make a small boy feel at home.

I was a bright child, apart from not being able to speak English, and soon started school. I attended an advanced learning class for kindergarten and worked on all sorts of neat things—blocks, letters, numbers and inter-gender communication. At least that's what I called it. In actuality, it just boiled down to trying to kiss as many girls on the bus as possible. For some reason, their reaction was less than enthusiastic. I guess I needed to do a little more studying—maybe I wasn't doing it right.

We moved a lot when I was growing up, and I found myself having to make new friends on a rather consistent basis. That wasn't too bad, but it seemed like I attracted kids that had some interesting characteristics. I guess I was just desperate. Or maybe all kids are like that at that age. One of my friends still wet his pants at the age of nine, another one made everyone call him "Chewbacca," and one girl even said she would show me what was under her clothes if I showed her what was under mine. Of course, what was under her clothes was a bathing suit. While I was wearing ONLY my bathing suit, and what was under was... Ahem, moving on. Strange, they may have been, but they were my friends, and as we ran

11

around on the playground imagining we were the "Dukes of Hazard," I was happy.

Grade school was an amalgamation of incredible boredom and extreme embarrassment. The classes weren't that hard, but the relationships were a killer. I had my first crush, kind of. Did you ever notice that it seems the people that you are attracted to never like you? At least that was how it was for me. I finally found a girl that expressed some interest. She wrote me one of those notes: "Do you like me? Check one: Yes, No, Maybe." I checked "maybe" because I wanted to hedge my bets, but from that time on, we were boyfriend and girlfriend. I was in heaven, until a week later, she dumped me for no apparent reason. Well, now that I think about it, I guess she must have had a reason. Maybe she was sick of me, maybe she liked someone else better, maybe she was just having a "bad hair day." It's amazing how anyone survives growing up without having homicidal tendencies.

I was a bit of a clumsy kid, but I played a couple of sports. I found out that I wasn't naturally talented, so I had to work harder than others. That was ok, I practiced a lot and became proficient at soccer and swimming. In eighth grade, I swam the breaststroke on the swim team. I did pretty well and the net result was that my chest was, as the body builders call it, "ripped." Of course the rest of me was as skinny as Kate Moss on Dexatrim, but as long as I kept a long baggy shirt and pants on, I looked well proportioned. Unfortunately, there were many moments of abject embarrassment as I was forced to reveal my chicken legs.

Fast forward to high school. Picture one very skinny Asian kid with huge glasses and white socks pulled up to his kneecaps, and you've pretty much got me pegged—socially inept, dressed in nerdy clothes, and trying to find who I was. Because my dad was a pastor, I may have felt the need to show off a bit, but I never got into any bad trouble—no gangs, drugs, or violence. Just the occasional grand theft auto with a side of bank robbery—not really, just wanted to keep you awake.

I did however make a habit out of sneaking out of my second story window, creeping along the outside window sill over to the stove pipe. I would then climb down the stove pipe, and run off with my friends into the cool night air. I'm not sure how God paid all the overtime for my guardian angels, but He protected us, and about the worst we ever did was to go down to the local 7/11 and get burritos. Pretty wild, huh?

Actually, one night I fell as I was moving to the stove pipe from the window. I lay there in the bushes groaning and hoping that my parents hadn't heard the loud crash. It was at that point that I began to realize that I needed to find other nocturnal activities to fill my time.

It was in college that my life did a fliparound. Even growing up in a pastor's home, I never really accepted God for my own. I knew a lot about God, but everything about Him was ritualistic. I said the Apostle's Creed, I went through catechism and I knew a lot of Bible stories. The problem was that they didn't mean much to me. Actually, they didn't mean anything to me. I was just walking out the empty words. It was in college that I started to believe for myself and asked Christ to play more than a bit part; and it was in college that I did the second most important thing of my life. I found my wife, Pam. In my freshman year.

I remember coming home from that year of school. I sat down with my parents and said: "I'm getting married." I watched as the inevitable look of panic stole over my parents' faces. They were sure that they were watching their only son make one of the biggest mistakes of his life—getting married too young. In their minds, it was only yesterday that they were changing my diapers and telling me to keep my mouth over my plate. Never mind the fact that I had braved the wilds of Africa, fought in two wars, spoke five languages, and was on the advisory committee to the Pope! Now, before you come off your seat in open-mouthed amazement at the achievements of my life at such a young age, I must tell you that I didn't do quite all of those things. Truthfully, I hadn't done any of those things. Maybe they had a point.

To my mother's credit her only words were: "Are you sure that's the right thing to do?" Of course I was sure! After all, I had been dating Pam for a whole month, and had been friends with her for a whole month before that, what else was there to do, but to get married? (Sense the sarcasm?) I was going to do what my parents were always telling me to do:

"Move out while I still knew everything." Now, I know that all the parents reading this are feeling your blood pressure rise as you think of your own children, but Pam and I were engaged for a year before the wedding, and I am not endorsing my life choices as appropriate for everyone. All that being said, everything worked out well for me in spite of myself.

God could not have chosen a better person for me—she complements my strengths, shores up my weaknesses, and loves me in spite of myself. Even though I was a bit young and more than a bit immature, God was not, and He chose someone who was so right for me, that had I waited until I was 237 years old, I still would not have attained enough knowledge to find such a good fit. OK, all parents, one big sigh of relief. Ready? Go.

Fast-forward to the present. I am now a pastor—yes, in spite of all the strangeness of growing up as an emotionally stunted son of a preacher-man. Someone once said that many times we become that which we most fear. (Actually, I think they said "If you keep making that face, it's going to freeze like that." But the principle still applies I think—work with me here.) Somewhere, buried deep in my psyche, there must have been a profound fear. A fear that I was unable to voice. A fear so innate, so ingrained, I didn't even know it was there—I must have been very afraid of being a pastor, because here I am.

I must have also been afraid of having two kids, because I am blessed with them as well. Truthfully, I was afraid of having twenty-seven kids, but thankfully that hasn't happened yet. (My apologies to those of you that have twenty-seven children and love every minute of it. Write me a letter and tell me how you do it!)

When I look at my life now and how God has blessed me—a wonderful wife, two great kids, a job that I love doing, two thriving businesses, a house to live in, and everything I need, one thing has become abundantly clear—God is faithful. When I look at my past and the stupid decisions that I made, the times that I thwarted the natural laws of the universe and laughed in the face of extreme danger, I know it's true—God is faithful. When I see the beautiful tapestry that He has woven out of my life in spite of all the times that I have picked at the threads of His plans, I feel it deep within the core of who I am—God is faithful!

Observations About God's Faithfulness

The faithfulness of God is an interesting thing. I began to keep a log of the ways that God was faithful to me. I would periodically go back and read the incidents to bolster my faith. I thought about the lessons that I learned through each incident—and there were two main things that I noticed about God. The first is that God's faithfulness never disappears, and the second is the purpose of His faithfulness.

God's Faithfulness Never Disappears

By nature of the definition of faithfulness, it never goes away; it never falters. It does not change. It doesn't go on vacation. It doesn't take a day off, it is faithful. Always there. Always able to be counted on. Its nature is to be solid, dependable, sunrise after sunset, from the time the moon waxes to the day that it begins to wane.

Take a look at your life. How many things are there that change from day to day? Even as I strive to have the same routine, things are constantly in motion. There is something in a human being though, that looks for that which is unchanging—that one point around which our world may revolve. As the planet around us moves, changes and seeks to hurt us, His faithfulness is the only centerpoint that never moves. I know that I will not wake up one day and find that God has decided that: "Today, I don't really feel like being faithful."

I can't tell you how much knowing this, not just in your head, but feeling it in your gut will change your perspective on life. You have to believe in the fact that God's faithfulness never disappears more than you trust in gravity. When that conviction is as embedded in you as flour is part of loaf of bread, you will be unafraid of change. You will look at each new day as an opportunity for success, not as a potential for colossal failure.

You will trust in God's plan in your life and you will trust that He wants what's best for you. When you hear Him directing, asking, pleading with you, you will step out with boldness, because in the protection of His faithfulness, there is no ultimate failure. The simple message is that in the end, you will win! Will you fall down along the way? Yes, of course, but He picks you up, dusts you off and turns your feet toward your next success, your next magnificent possibility. See, his faithfulness is the safety net. Yes, we still fall, and yes, it does sting a bit (or a lot), but His faithfulness always catches us before we reach terminal velocity.

In the past, I have confused the faithfulness of God with getting what I wanted. So if things were hard, or something bad happened my question was: "Where was God's faithfulness?" But the thing that I have learned is this—it hadn't disappeared, I had misinterpreted what form His faithfulness would take. Just because my definition of faithfulness is wrong, it does not mean that God is not faithful. I am learning to see that God is close and true even when I don't get what I want. And sometimes, He is especially trustworthy in not letting me have what I desire. I'm not the sharpest knife in the drawer!

Sometimes, though, we doubt His dependability. We see how he has "failed" in the life of someone we care about or in our own life and ask; "How can God be faithful and allow this to happen?" There are no easy answers to this question, only a choice. You choose to believe that God is faithful, that He has a plan, that the end of the story isn't written, that what Satan meant for evil, God will turn to good, and draw close to Him, or you choose to walk away.

Take the story of Joseph. Talk about hard times. Talk about a reason to doubt the faithfulness of God! But he didn't. Every time something bad happened to Joseph—when he was sold into slavery or thrown in jail for doing what was right, he made the choice to believe in a faithful God.

I'm sure it wasn't easy for him, sitting in a dark, stinky cell under false accusation. I'm sure he had doubts, but he made the choice to believe that God would come through.

God's faithfulness does not go away in hard times; it is proved in hard times. In the Great Commission in Matthew, Jesus says "And surely I am with you always, to the very end of the age." (Matt. 28:20 NIV) Period. The end. My belief in God's faithfulness does not make God trustworthy or not—but many times, it helps me to handle the situation much better.

I have noticed that when I am going through hard times, if I trust in God's faithfulness, I cope with the difficulty much more smoothly. On the other hand, when I forget about the truth of how He has come through in the past, the situation overwhelms me and causes quite a squirrelly mess.

God, by His nature is faithful. Though all of the things around us change. Even if the mountains fall into the seas. Despite our belief or doubt. When everyone we know and care about turns against us. When we can't trust our feelings, our faith, our friends, our finances, or our fate, God is faithful. Period.

The Purpose of God's Faithfulness

God created us for relationship. He does not demand us to come close to Him, because that's not the type of relationship that He wants—one built on fear and obligation. He humbly asks that we would get to know Him; that we would draw close to Him. He provides such never-ending dedication to show us that we can trust Him. His faithfulness is there, never failing, just so that we would come into a close relationship with Him.

God is faithful. He always has been, He always will be. Unfortunately, we have a hard time believing that sometimes. We think "How could God be so devoted to me when I have turned my back on Him so many times?" We condemn the Peter in us that has turned away from the love of Christ. And we try harder. But we do it out of guilt. We try to earn God's favor with our dedication to church, to "His Work," to reading our Bible.

These are all good things, but in the end, if done for the wrong reasons, they drive us farther from the purpose of God's faithfulness, not toward it. Just as a parent with a child, God teaches us that we can depend on Him. He will always be there for us. He wants to teach us how to "catch a ball," he wants to dry our eyes when we've had our hearts broken.

If you are a parent, think about how it feels to have your child come up to you, wrap their arms around you, and whisper into your ear; "I love you!" That's what God wants—that heartfelt relationship with us. He realizes though, that in order to foster that, it requires Him to be there for us each and every time we "fall down and skin our knee."

God requests faithfulness from us, but He requires that our loyalty springs from a love relationship with Him, rather than guilt over what we are doing or not doing.

If you are struggling with the faithfulness of God and you are feeling guilt because you know that you are not faithful to Him, do not try to assuage the guilt by "making" yourself be devoted. This is something I constantly fight against. It springs from that part in me that wants to "perform." I found that when I build the type of love relationship with Him that He desires, my faithfulness toward Him comes naturally as I begin to see the way He loves me. That is the only way it works.

The Bible tells us that God makes the first move when it comes to loving us—when it comes to being faithful to us. Romans 5:8 says "But God demonstrates his own love for us in this: While we were still sinners, Christ died for us." (NIV) And in 2 Timothy 2:13 it says "if we give up on Him, He does not give up—for there's no way He can be false to Himself." (MSG)

God's faithfulness is something that He does to build relationship with you—not something to try to guilt you into being devoted to Him.

Take a look at my life. No puzzle piece has been left out. As you read the following stories, you will see how some of them are made up of so many different pieces, but in the right time at the right place, God brought all of those pieces together; and the end result was so much more than I could have imagined. In every area that I have trusted Him, there has been peace and joy. It's not that my family and I don't go through hard times, we do. But in the hardest places, the darkest corners and the most treacherous journeys, God has truly been faithful.

Bikes and Testosterone

Did you ever notice that Springtime tends to bring out the stupidity in men? Or maybe it just brings out the stupidity in me. It could just be the fact that I live in Michigan. To say that the winters here are long would be like saying that B.B. King could play a guitar a little bit. Or that the Sears Tower is "kind of a tall building." Winters here seem longer than it would take to fly to Mars—on a bicycle.

Long and cold. So, in the eyes of a normal Michigander (no joke, that's what we call ourselves—or is it Michiganian, I forget,) spring is like the final bell on the final day of your final year of high school. It is a time to throw away all restraint and wallow in the ecstasy of not having to wear 40 pounds of fur. It is a time to celebrate the coming of something that you were sure was never going to arrive. It is new hope, new possibilities, new promises of stupidity.

I was caught up in the thralls of spring and decided that I wanted to try mountain biking. Maybe it was the television commercials that showed dirt-covered guys bleeding from both legs as they tumbled pell-mell down a cliff. In my spring-addled brain, I must have thought that looked cool. Or maybe I was just tired of having the use of all my limbs and full capacity of thought.

So, I got a mountain bike in my eternal quest to be "with it." I shopped long and hard, looking for something that could be used for aggressive biking, but didn't drain my already thin wallet. I didn't want shocks because they took away some of the energy from every pedal stroke, I couldn't afford aluminum, so I ended up with a good off-road bike with tires that would rip up the pavement.

I didn't want to be one of those lame bikers, though, that had a super-cool, tricked out, extreme bike but never took it to any place more exciting than the local Winn-Dixie. After all, the TV commercials never show someone riding to the store, they are always out in the Sierra Nevada's challenging rock formations. I lived in town though, and we had no huge rock formations, so I decided to challenge myself by riding some of the local nature trails.

Trail cycling is different than riding on a street as you could probably guess. It takes quick thinking, fast reflexes, and a certain amount of insanity. Well, I rode my bike without incident for a couple of weeks and was building strength—more than enough, I thought, to compete with some of the aerobatic antics of professional riders. So, I took the next step. I went to some trails located near my house that were a little more extreme. Well, "near" is a relative word—they were about four miles away. To be clear, I was not an expert rider and had not trained extensively—no matter what I thought, so eight miles was a good day's ride for me. But the beautiful spring somehow told me that I could ride 16 miles that day. It lied to me.

I got to the trails, and rode around a bit. These paths ran for miles right next to a ravine. They curved around small bushes and up and down gentle hills. Everywhere you looked, there were tall grasses and wildflowers. The colors of spring had done themselves proud and the lure of unexplored wilderness called to me with its siren song. I explored with reckless abandon and enjoyed the ride on the mild swells. Then I got cocky.

There was a trail that led to the bottom of the ravine and emptied out onto a nice winding pathway along the creek there. That lone path was the only safe way to get to the bottom of the gorge. Everywhere else, a cliff separated the top of the ravine from the bottom. This precipice dropped 50 feet straight down. The top jutted out, then was undercut for about 16 feet. Finally, the bottom stuck out slightly. The entire drop-off was covered with hardened sand, dirt, and rocks.

Eventually, I found myself at the top of that cliff. Maybe it was the fresh spring breeze blowing through my hair, maybe it was my overdeveloped sense of freedom, but something told me that it would be a good idea to ride my bike off the top of the cliff. I would free fall about 20 feet, then land almost vertical on the escarpment, gracefully steering past rocks and debris to stop at the bottom in a cloud of dust, raising my fist triumphantly in the air to celebrate my manhood! Unfortunately, my mind was writing checks my body couldn't cash.

You see, we had been blessed with a torrential downpour a couple of days before I went riding. It was dry now, but it had left hard rivulets in the cliff where the water had rushed madly down in its hurry to get to the bottom. In the loftiness of my vision, I had failed to see these, failed to account for them, failed to think through the disastrous results that they would bring. Blithely, I turned my bike to the chasm, pedaled forward and soared through the air.

My carefree flight through the air lasted about a half a second. When I hit the ground, my front tire found the nearest crevasse, stuck, and sent me sliding down the cliff. I tried to grab onto anything that I could to stop my death plunge down the precipice. Failing that, I tried to disentangle my legs, arms and head from my bike. Realizing that, too was a lost cause, I opted to lay down on my side and rear end and allow the hill to sandpaper my bare skin to shiny smoothness. Fun, huh?

I came to a stop in a cloud of dust a bit dazed and confused. It had not gone exactly as I had planned. It had gone so far afield from what I had envisioned in fact, that I was afraid to move.

Well, as I lay there at the bottom of my stupidity groaning in agony, I took a mental assessment of my body—no broken bones, my head had been protected by my helmet, and no memory loss; I could remember every moment of my fateful tumble. However, I had given the hill about 65% of the skin that used to cover the right side of my body.

They say that in the moments before death, your life flashes before your eyes. I don't know if that is true, but I can tell you that as I lay in the dirt at the bottom of that cliff, I could sense things more clearly. I could almost hear the wind whistling through the wings of the hawk as it soared. I marveled at the way the clouds formed shapes and patterns that were all unique, all different. And I was very aware of each and every nerve, muscle, bone, tendon and skin cell in my right side—because they felt like they had been dipped in gasoline and set on fire.

I realized that lying there pondering the wonder of God's creation wasn't going to get me the giant band-aid that I needed, so I slowly pushed myself off the ground—bruised, bleeding and yes, more than a bit demoralized at the obvious lack of "coolness" that I had exhibited. I took a moment to allow the dizziness to pass, and then I achingly gathered my bike, which fared much better than I did, and set off on the four-mile bike ride toward home. I've noticed that I tend to ride much faster when I am not skinned like a chicken and so the four-mile ride seemed like forty. Inch-by-painful-inch, I moved toward home.

At the time, my wife Pam and I lived in a little two-bedroom college apartment on the second floor. The kitchenette had four cupboards and two burners on the stove. Really. The bedrooms were about the size of your bathroom, and the entire affair had all the charm of a fallout shelter, complete with cement block walls. The building was built in the sixties, meant for two-year temporary use. But, as with most educational institutions, here it was, over 30 years later and still standing—barely.

I got back to my apartment, limped up the concrete stairs, and was met with an unpleasant surprise. I had no keys. I knew they were in my pocket when I left the house before the fateful ride. But alas, there were no keys in my pocket now! As I began to search my mind for where I could have lost them, I inevitably came to the same conclusion that you already have. I lost them on the cliff! My options were limited. I couldn't even crawl in the window because even if I could have somehow jumped past the first floor, stuck to the wall like Spider Man and made it to the opening, these were the type that only opened eight inches. Admittedly I was somewhat skinnier then, but not quite that skinny.

After sitting down, wallowing in self-pity for a moment and exhausting all possible options, I realized that I would have to go back to the cliff and try to find the errant keys. I cannot tell you the warmth and cheer this beautiful thought brought to me! I was bruised. I was bloody. I was exhausted. I looked like a very underdone cut of veal. I was in no shape to go back out there. There was no other option though, so I began the journey.

The ride back to the scene of my embarrassment was grueling—made all the more so by knowledge that the possibility of finding my keys was smaller than the likelihood of a seven year old growing a beard and dancing the Macarena. As I stood in front of the cliff and saw the immense area that I was going to have to cover, my heart sank. The marks where I fell were embedded in the face, and they did not go straight down. Add that to the fact that much of the overhang was now loose sand, and I began to realize the keys could have been anywhere in a 700 square foot area and buried up to a foot-and-a-half deep in the dirt. My heart fell.

I felt that I would surely have to wait the six hours until my wife got home from work. Actually, at that point, I would have welcomed such an easy release. She would find me curled up in a ball on the front stoop unconscious from loss of blood. This probably was not the best way to greet my wonderful wife after a hard day of work, but I was beyond caring. I just wanted to pass out so that I wouldn't feel any more pain. Thankfully, God had different plans.

Forgetting that God said in His Word that if we sought Him, He would be found by us (Jeremiah 29:13 NIV), and that He cares for us (Nahum 1:7 NIV), I crawled up and down that cliff for over a half an hour. I had reached the point of despair, I was bloody, and the footprints I made had pretty much obliterated all hope of ever finding the keys. Then God had mercy on me and a thought came into my head: "This would go a lot easier with God involved." So I prayed. I wish I could say that I was eloquent and spoke a spiritually moving prayer complete with "thee's" and "thou's," but I think my prayer sounded more like this:

"God, help! I need to find my keys! I don't want to die in the middle of nowhere, cold and alone while the bears feast on my flesh! Thanks." Obviously, that was an exaggeration, it was spring. I wasn't cold.

After that intensely spiritual prayer I turned around. I put my foot down and stepped on my keys! I would have whooped and yelled and jumped up and down, but I was just too tired so I bypassed the wild celebrating. Looking back at my physical state at that point, I can honestly say that was probably my wisest decision that day. I settled for thanking the Lord all the way home and limping into my apartment, to begin the laborious task of bandaging my many wounds.

Well, the scars have long since faded from that incident, but the knowledge that I gleaned from that experience with God is still with me. I learned a valuable lesson about God's faithfulness that day.

God Cares About Small Things Too

God cares about the small things like keys. He cared that I was standing there on the side of a cliff, skinned like a fish looking for them. He knew where they were, and He cared enough about me to show me. Up until that fateful day on the bluff, I tended to think of God as someone that was needed for big things like life-threatening illnesses and world hunger. I would call on Him only in those times when my fat was entirely in the fire and there was no other option. I don't know, maybe I thought that small things were too insignificant to bother Him with, but for whatever reason, I thought that I could and should only bring "things worthy of His attention" to Him. Make no mistake, He cares very deeply about those things. But God also cares about the small things. This is key. (Get it? It's a play on the word "key" like the keys I lost that day, and also key meaning important…oh never mind.)

The reason it is so imperative to know beyond the shadow of a doubt that God cares about small things is because if we can't conceive of a God that cares about small things, no matter how hard we try, we will never be able to believe that God cares about big things. I know that some of you are out there saying that you know that God cares about big things. It's not a matter of just caring though. The reason we need God to care about our problems, whether big or small is because we need Him to act—to be able and willing to do something about them. And if we are to believe that He will move in all the areas of our lives, we need to be convinced He cares about our difficulties—even the problems we think are too small to "bother Him with."

See, this type of confidence is not just thinking that something might happen, or thinking that God is able to do something. This type of belief is the kind of "suck in your gut, and step off the cliff" type that requires action. When we truly have confidence that God is going to act on our behalf, no matter what the situation, it changes the way that we think about the problem, the actions we take, the way we talk and the entire way we go about our lives. Trust that deep only comes from a lifetime of proving that God cares about small things.

For example, I found that I couldn't be convinced that God was going to provide for a $12,000 deficit in our finances unless I could believe that God cared about the five dollars I lost on the way to the mall. In the same way that you wouldn't expect a child learning to walk to run a marathon, God doesn't expect us to trust Him for seemingly impossible situations right away. God cares about all things. Big or small, important or seemingly unimportant. Experiencing this care is what builds our faith.

And when our faith is built up, anything is possible with God. Look at the verse that says: "If you have faith like a mustard seed, you can say to the mountain "be removed" and it will cast itself into the sea." (Matt. 17:20 NIV) Conversely, if we don't have faith, we close ourselves off to the supernatural working of God in our lives. Take for example Matthew 13:58 where it says "And he did not do many miracles there, because of their lack of faith." (NIV)

When you begin to have faith like a mustard seed your certainty is deep enough to make a difference in your life. Reread the verse about the mustard seed. If you will notice, faith alone isn't enough. You have to couple it with action—you have to "say to the mountain 'be removed.'"

I'm not talking about something "spookinatural" here, I'm talking about a trust in God's faithfulness strong enough that you are willing to do what that faith requires.

Look for those small things where God was true and constant in your life. Find his faithfulness. When I have done that, I realize that my trust in God in those small things has prepared me for the next step that God had for me.

Because God was faithful in a small thing like the key incident, when something bigger came up, I was able to rely on Him in that. Luke 12: 22-31 talks about worry. In verse 24 it says; "Consider the ravens: They do not sow or reap, they have no storeroom or barn; yet God feeds them." (NIV) God feeds them. This verse almost makes it sound like God holds out his hands with food for the ravens. I can picture the ravens perching on His fingers and eating out of His hands.

This gives us a view of God that is caring, gentle, and yes, very concerned about the small things. Since that time on the hill, I have not hesitated to bring anything to God. Everything from feeling a cold coming on to incredible hardship and heartache find His ears. I am in no way perfect, or have this faith thing down pat, but when situations are at their worst, I perch on His able hands while he feeds me. (But I don't eat worms or birdseed for that matter.)

There was one last thing that I learned that day. This didn't have a whole lot to do with God, but it was a good lesson nonetheless. If you are standing at the top of a cliff with the aspiration to soar with the eagles, don't.

Buying the Boy

My wife wanted a child. To me a child was like a good burrito, I wouldn't mind having one, but it wouldn't change my evening all that much—except to give me gas. I know, I know, incredibly self-absorbed, huh? Welcome to the true thought patterns of a man. I actually wanted a child as well, but not as much as I wanted to practice making a child. (If you are underage, please go back one sentence and delete it from your memory banks.)

One thing that was very important to me though, was making my wife happy. I knew that she had a void that could only be filled by raising a child. I thought I might make a decent dad as well, so after thinking about it for a while, I was 110% on board with the whole baby train and ready to leave the station. I want to be clear that I wasn't just doing this for Pam, I really did have a desire to have a child, I just didn't see any rush to have it before my eightieth birthday. After a careful study of human physiology, though, I realized that unless my name was Abraham, this was highly improbable, so I changed my mind and decided that there was no time like the present.

Pam and I happily tried to have a child for over a year, but no results. Well, this was a bit disconcerting. She wanted four kids and I was tabulating the length of time that it was taking just to make one.

Extrapolating from the present timetable, I figured that by the time we had four kids, they would have to change my diapers, not the other way around. Oh well.

I wanted two kids. My wife came from a family that had five children. My family had my sister and I. I had been with her family for holidays. I liked our version better. I am not against large families, they make great football teams. But my preference was for a smaller family. In the end, it was immaterial since we were both willing to compromise. The way that it was going though, my wife and I would have to act like children instead of raising our own, and we would have to take turns dressing up in the bonnet and riding in the stroller. Not a great situation.

One night as we took a walk together, enjoying the cool night air and lost in the bliss of the twinkling stars, she looked at me with those beautiful blue eyes and said: "Let's get help." I started looking around frantically trying to find someone that was being mugged, but she went on to explain that she wanted to go to an infertility specialist. Yea.

There is nothing as fun in any man's mind as his wife suggesting that he go to a place that will put his masculinity on trial—and probably find it lacking. I suppose it may rank right up there with having major surgery. Without anesthetic. I'm not sure which is worse: being in a place where the purpose is to find out what is wrong with you, or recognizing that everyone in the vicinity knows you're shooting blanks.

Infertility clinics are strange places. They are mauve colored torture chambers of great insecurity. The whole time you are sweating and wondering if there is something wrong with you. To make yourself feel better, you begin to trash-talk the other people in the waiting room in your mind. As you sit there, you look at the other people and smile and nod to them. Inwardly, you think: "How are you, sterile person?" and "Oh, she's nice looking, too bad she's barren." And then you look over to your right and there is a woman with a baby. And you think: "I'll bet you that baby isn't even hers, she just brought it along to throw the rest of us off." I know, it sounds mean, but that's what happens. Then you realize they are doing the same thing to you. Suddenly, trash talk isn't as much fun.

Then the "evil nurse from the planet Zoltron" calls your name. She disguises her diabolical plan with a smile and soothing words. She brings you into a back room, takes your temperature, hits your knees with a hammer (I'm still not sure what that has to do with your ability to conceive a child) and hands you a plastic cup. The entire consultation is an exercise in humility. You are poked, prodded, and asked questions that couldn't be repeated in mixed company.

This wonderful event culminates in a humiliating meeting with a kindly doctor who oh, so gently tells you: "You can't have a child." You think to yourself: "He went to medical school for how long? I KNOW I CAN'T HAVE A CHILD! Why do you think I'm here?" It's like going up to a feline and saying "I have been thinking long and hard about this and I think that I have come to a conclusion. You are a cat." To which she would reply "Puuuuurrrr." If you made a habit of telling cats that, soon someone would knock on the door carrying a nice white coat with very long sleeves to remind you of your appointment with a padded cell.

In order to redeem himself in your eyes, the doctor rattles of a list of problems that either you, your partner, or both of you may or may not have. Interestingly enough, most of these end in "osis."

Thankfully, there were things wrong with both my wife and myself. Wait, that came out wrong! Oh well, that's what I meant. See, if there was only something wrong on my end, I would feel horrible. But I guess misery loves company because I felt a lot better that we were in this together. I know, I know, I'm incredibly shallow.

The funny thing about the whole meeting was that even though the doctor said we couldn't have a child, he still wanted money. He went on to say that there was a series of procedures that we could do that would increase our chance of having a baby. These items started out with a price tag of about $3,000 and went up to about $15,000. I felt like I was at a really expensive boutique store and the salesperson was showing me the merchandise. You would think that for $15,000, there would be a written guarantee and they would operate on you with gold instruments—but guess what? I asked the doctor what the chance of us getting pregnant with the expensive procedure was and his answer was basically: "Better than without it."

However, Pam and I talked, and we decided that we wanted to go down this road. I mean who wouldn't want to spend a bunch of money on something that you didn't know would work? We didn't actually want to go down the road, we just wanted the baby at the end, but you get the drift. So began a wonderful and exciting journey! Can you smell the sarcasm?

We began what seemed like a merry-go-round of wearing certain types of clothes, and planning down to the minute times we would be together. We got on the roller coaster of excitement when we would think she was pregnant, only to plunge into the steaming dragons' mouth of despair when we found she wasn't. And we played the rigged carnival games of having procedures done to increase our chances.

One year, three months, seven days, two hours and four minutes this went on. Well, if I'm honest, I'm not really sure exactly how long we went through that process, but I do remember when it stopped.

We were on vacation in Florida. We were walking on a sandbar and talking as the sea lapped at our feet. (Don't worry, we didn't get stung by any jellyfish.) By the way, if you are looking for a good place to contemplate a large decision, or the takeover of a small country, I would definitely recommend this setting. It is so peaceful. Anyway, we looked lovingly at each other and both said "I'm done." Pam knew what I was talking about and I understood what she was saying. We were done being poked and prodded, wondering each month if this would be the month only to find that it wasn't. We wanted to move on. We wanted to live life.

For us that meant adoption. Pam and I had talked about adoption before and said that someday we would like to adopt. As I mentioned before, I was adopted and was very thankful that I was, so this was a natural fit. I guess that I thought we would adopt after we had kids born from our bodies. If this meant that I got to skip the fertility doctor though, I was all for it.

So we happily went to the adoption agency and started the process. We just didn't know what we were in for. If the screening for bearing a child was a rigorous as the one for adopting a child, there would be a lot less unplanned pregnancies. I think that by the end of the home study, the only thing that the adoption agency didn't know about me was the color of my chewing gum. And since I stuck a few pieces under the chair I was sitting in, chances are, they knew that as well.

I won't say that this undertaking was any easier than the fertility doctor, but at least we were making progress. We went through the home study process, paid a lot of money and then we waited. And waited some more. I was beginning to wonder what it would be like to have a baby in the nursing home. Then we finally got the call. There was a beautiful baby boy waiting for his new family. We finally had our child.

When we started adoption, one of the things that Pam was really excited about was that she wouldn't have to go though labor. She was wrong. Pam went through one of the hardest labors of anyone I know— twenty-two hours on a plane with a six-month-old baby that she had just met. When I greeted them at the airport, she started crying. I thought she was ecstatic at seeing me, but it turns out she just had to go to the bathroom.

Thus started our happy family. And as I held that little wiggling baby boy in my arms, I knew that my hopes for a son, my dreams to start a family were complete. God had chosen our child, brought him halfway around the world and put him into my arms at that moment. And as he wrapped his hand around my finger, I could tell he knew that I was his dad.

You may ask; "How was God faithful in this situation? You still weren't able to have a baby. You didn't get your wish." My answer is this: "God was more faithful in this situation than He has been in almost any other circumstance in my life." See, in this situation, God saved me from myself. I had a plan. I was implementing the plan. But, I dread to think what would have happened if I would have gotten my plan and not His.

If I would have gotten my plan, our baby may have died, or been sick, or Pam could have had problems with the pregnancy. But most of all, I would have missed out on the amazing feeling I get each time I look at Caleb and call him "son." There was some reason that God decided to do things in this way. I am content to trust that He knew best and was watching my back the whole time.

Our Adoption

Through this experience, God taught me what it was like to be adopted into His family. You see, I had experienced it from the other side. Because I was adopted when I was young, I knew what it was like to come into a family, to be unconditionally loved, to be treasured and treated like a son. This taught me what it was like from God's point of view.

From the time we brought Caleb home, people have teased me saying that I must have gone to Korea and sowed some wild oats because we look and act so much like each other. He likes to do many of the same things I like doing, he likes the same foods I like, he even talks like me. It is a natural fit. Our family had a space in it that was shaped just like him. It didn't matter that he didn't come from Pam's womb. God made him to fit into our family.

It is the same way with each of us. God made us to fit into His family. In the same way that Caleb's life would have been a lot different, a lot less complete if he would have had to have grown up in an orphanage in South Korea, we are much less complete if we "stay in the orphanage" and don't allow ourselves to be gathered into our natural home.

Every time I look into Caleb's eyes, I know that God brought him halfway around the world just because He knew that only Pam and I could raise him to be the man of God that he needs to be. That only we could be the parents he needs. God's got great plans for our kids and each day I feel humbled and privileged to be a part of that. And the awesome part is that God has great plans for each one of you as His children. Every time Caleb holds my hand and calls me dad, there is no doubt in my mind that God fulfilled our wish and brought us our son.

Psalm 139:1-16 says:

"O LORD, you have searched me
and you know me.
You know when I sit and when I rise;
you perceive my thoughts from afar.

You discern my going out and my lying down;
you are familiar with all my ways.
Before a word is on my tongue
you know it completely, O LORD.
You hem me in—behind and before;
you have laid your hand upon me.
Such knowledge is too wonderful for me,
too lofty for me to attain.
Where can I go from your Spirit?
Where can I flee from your presence?
If I go up to the heavens, you are there;
if I make my bed in the depths, you are there.
If I rise on the wings of the dawn,
if I settle on the far side of the sea,
even there your hand will guide me,
your right hand will hold me fast.
If I say, "Surely the darkness will hide me
and the light become night around me,"
even the darkness will not be dark to you;
the night will shine like the day,
for darkness is as light to you.
For you created my inmost being;
you knit me together in my mother's womb.
I praise you because I am fearfully and wonderfully made;
your works are wonderful,
I know that full well.
My frame was not hidden from you
when I was made in the secret place.
When I was woven together in the depths of the earth,
your eyes saw my unformed body.
All the days ordained for me
were written in your book
before one of them came to be." (NIV)

See, God knows you. He created you, and He created you with one purpose in mind—to be adopted by Him. He created you to be part of His family and to have a relationship with Him. If our lives have other goals that take precedence over knowing God—like fame, money, security or lust, we will always feel empty, searching. The ultimate point of our existence is to know God and be adopted as His son or daughter. And when we become part of His family and spend time with Him, we start to take on His attributes, we begin to act like Him.

Have you ever thought about what an amazing thing it is that the King of all creation wants us to be His sons and daughters? I guess it would be kind of like Bill Gates landing his helicopter in your back yard and telling you that he would like you to be a part of his family. If you accept, you have access to all the family money—without limit; you can use the private jet to go wherever you want, and all of the Gates' fortune and pull in industry would back you up in whatever you decide to do.

It's the same thing (to a much, much lesser degree) with Caleb. Because he is part of our family, he has access to all the resources that we have. Our fortune will someday be his and if anyone messes with him, guess what? It ticks me off, and I jump to his aid!

God owns everything. He has the right of ownership because He created it—He holds all of the patents if you will. Psalm 8:3 says "When I consider your heavens, the work of your fingers, the moon and the stars, which you have set in place..." He owns the stars, the planets, the air, the grass, the money, the buildings—everything but you and I. The reason that He doesn't own us is because He has granted us free will.

When we choose to become part of His family, all of the things that He owns become ours as well. Could you imagine waking up one day and asking your dad for a planet? How about some property on Mars? Well, with God, that is actually a possibility. That is the type of power that He has. His resources are inexhaustible. So many times we limit our thinking about what we can or cannot do to the things we can accomplish by ourselves. We forget that we have the backing of our "dad" behind us.

That is not to say that we can get anything we want—because just like with our parenting of Caleb, we don't let him have things that aren't good for him. We love him too much to let him harm himself. When he goes after those things that are in his best interest, though, we put unimaginable effort into making sure that he achieves his goals.

In our adoption, God brings all those things to the table—power, authority, money, eternal life. What do we bring to the relationship? Our love. God longs to be with us, just like, without knowing it, I longed to be with my son. He longs for us to love Him, wholly, unreservedly, and without shame. My heart melts when Caleb, holding my hand, looks up at me, hugs my leg and says "You're the best dad in the whole world!" I take him into my arms and tell him how much he means to me. And just like Caleb fills the missing place in our family, you fill the missing place in God's heart. He longs to take you into His arms, tell you how much He loves you and welcome you home.

Which House?

Studies have shown that buying a house is one of the top ten stresses in life. It's right up there with having surgery and death. I can vouch for the validity of these studies having moved over 12 times in my life and buying several houses. This is a story about the strange way we bought our second house.

We had started a business in our home. It didn't begin that way. I had only wanted to be my own boss, and so I started doing freelance design work. It grew from there. We lived in a quiet three-bedroom ranch at the end of a cul-de-sac. It was white with pale blue shutters and had no grass in the back yard (lots of weeds, though). I mowed the weeds anyway, so they wouldn't feel left out on mowing day. The back yard was fenced by a grove of pine trees. The neighborhood was only about 15 houses, and the people were friendly and close knit. It was a common occurrence to see kids riding their bikes around, or families going for a walk together. If you saw your neighbor, you would stop and talk—maybe about life, maybe about kids, or maybe about what your other neighbors were doing—gossip, in other words.

The business was growing past the point that one person could handle it and still remain on the correct side of the door to a padded cell, so I hired a high school student to help with errands and things. That wasn't enough, so I hired a designer. That wasn't enough, so I hired another designer. At that point, the small bedroom that we were working in began to smell like feet and I was afraid one of the employees would sue me for having a hostile working environment.

In order to gain more space, we renovated the basement and turned it into an office area. We put in wood floors, a conference room, a reception area, and a designer's work area. Finally, enough room we thought. But a problem arose. There were people everywhere in our small, quiet home. They were there when we woke up in the morning, they were there when we took a nap, they were there late at night—because the advertising business is not a nine-to-five job. It got to the point that my wife and I felt guilty when we wanted to take a day off. We felt like prisoners. All we needed were the orange jumpsuits to make our incarceration complete.

To top it off, we had a small child. I think this is the stuff that great jokes are made of. "What do you get when you put two designers, an office manager, two parents, and a toddler in the same house…" We knew we had to do something about the situation, so Pam and I decided to move to a new house and leave the business in the old house. Actually, we prayed about it before we made the decision, but things were so desperate that I would have had a very serious conversation with God if His answer would have been "No."

The plan was that we would sell the business and move. The designer that had been with us the longest was interested in buying, so it was an easy decision. We would sell the business, the designer and his wife would rent the home, we would buy a different house and all would be well—said the idealistic, naive perfectionist!

So we began the task of looking for that perfect house. Now finding the perfect house is not as easy a task as you might think—if you want to spend less than the Gross National Product. After much brow-beating, we decided that we would buy land and then put a modular home on it. I've found that building or ordering a home is an interesting experience, because you want everything to be perfect. I guess the thought process is: "If I'm going to spend the money on this house, it had better be right." So, you move a wall here or there. You order the better appliances, you upgrade the carpet and counter tops. Pretty soon you are past the limit of your budget and crying "Uncle!"

After we had settled on a home with over 1900 first floor square feet, we began our journey to find land. Like the explorers of long ago, we braved hardships beyond endurance, crossed raging waters and fought savage indigenous tribes. Oh wait, that's a different book. Actually, we did end up looking at many different pieces of land, but never found something that was just perfect. It either had too many trees, or not enough trees, or was too expensive, you know the drill. We finally found one that we thought would work. Now I am going to give you the secret to a happy and successful life: notice the phrase I used above: "we thought would work," and as you seek to follow God's will in your life, avoid it like 12 day-old-pork rinds. Presto, instant happiness!

The six acres that we picked out was not perfect. It was not something that you would see in *Better Homes and Gardens*, it was something you would see in *Farm and Garden*. And it would have cows on it. The end of the land backed up to a creek that adjoined the piece of property. It had many small rolling hills that would be acceptable for the walk-out basement that we were planning. And it had one tree. Just one. I should mention that the tree was a giant oak that stood off to one side of the property—but it was still, no matter how you try to brush it up, just one tree.

We made an offer on the land. We finalized the plans for the house and made a down payment. We secured the financing. We signed the contract with the person who was going to buy the business. We breathed a sigh of relief because the plan was in motion. (Notice how many "we's" there are in these sentences?)

And then, one by one, all of our plans began to fall apart. When we had prayed about it, we felt God was in agreement with the move, and He was, but His plans for the final result were much different than we expected!

The offer we made on the land was accepted and we began to move forward. The property had no available sewer and water, so we had to put in a septic system and a well. That's when we found out that the entire piece of land that we had purchased was made of clay. There was no place on the property for a septic system. They would have to bring in sand and build it. I began to talk to different people about this, and many of them had stories of loved ones or acquaintances that had put in that type of system before and had been paying the price for years. Then the people in charge of the septic told me the price. It was going to be $10,000 more to do things this way. I was at the limit of my budget with just the purchase of the land and house, I could not afford to pay $10,000 more.

So, we went to the place that was going to build our home to see if there was anything else we could do. "No," they said, "it will cost $10,000 more." We had put about $8,000 dollars down on the house. We asked if we could get that refunded. They said they would have to get back to us on that. I didn't hold out much hope.

Meanwhile, profits from the business had dried up. Our billings were down about 60% per month for three months running. I looked at the future projects and they were even more sparse than what we had going on at the time. I knew I couldn't sell the business this way—it would never survive. And because the business sale agreement was that I would receive a percentage of the profits for the next several years, it was very important that the business did well!

I had applied for a professorship at one of the local universities. This was what I had chosen as my next career path. I could picture myself feeding young minds with the same drivel that I was fed. I'm sorry, did I say drivel? I meant "important knowledge." I would teach design and wear a beret and read poetry on the weekends. Alas, it was not to be! After a lengthy interview process, I found out that I did not get the position. Instead they went with someone that had more teaching experience.

As I pondered that job after-the-fact though, I realized that I wouldn't have been happy doing it. Yes, it would have put food on the table and would have paid well, but I would have not been achieving anything but tenure. I came to the understanding that with the type of personality that God gave me, I had to be building something that is so big that there is no way that I could accomplish it. I had to be daily challenged and stretched to perform beyond my potential. I would have done that job, all the while frustrated, mired in the bureaucracy and unrelenting sameness of academia.

With everything falling apart, the business sale in danger of not going through and my chosen career path no longer an option, we went back to the seller of the property and tried to back out of the deal. That was not possible according to him. (And according to the contract we signed. I guess that's why you have to sign a contract, so that people can't back out of them.) Being reasonable people, we asked nicely and said "Please!" For some reason, his answer was still "No!" and he threatened to take us to court if we did not fulfill the obligations of the contract. This was not turning out the way that we had envisioned!

So let's recap. Our grand scheme to move to the country, build our own home, and sell the business was in shambles. We were in danger of being sued. Our neighbors were angry with us because of the amount of traffic that went in and out of our driveway. And to top it off, I would not be able to be a professor and wear a beret. Drat!

We decided to press on. What else could we do? We called our realtor and asked about other properties that were on the market. She told us about another property that was located just outside of town and had been listed the day before we inquired. We went to view the house and our jaws dropped—but it wasn't from excitement. The house was mustard color and smelled like mold. The inside had orange shag carpeting and dark brown veneer cupboards. The screen porch housed more dead flies than a plague and in the back yard was a 50' pole with guide wires draping from the top to various points in the yard. One good thing though, was that there was not one but two thirty-five foot television towers—one on either end of the house! Great, huh?

The land, though, that was a different story. It was idyllic. There was a ravine with trees; there were two ponds, a meadow, and about fifty apple trees throughout the twenty acres. The best part is that this house, including the land was about $50,000 less than we were going to spend on the six acres and building a home. We could fix up the house and save ourselves $30,000.

Convincing your wife that it is a good idea to give up a new home with 3800 square feet and move into an 1100 square foot home with orange shag carpeting is rather like dipping your hand in meat sauce and petting a hungry lion. It is definitely not something that I would recommend doing without proper training. Actually, it didn't take that much convincing, though, because Pam could readily see that enormous potential of the land and loved the views from the windows of the house. So, we made an offer.

Meanwhile, we still hadn't gotten out of our previous house deal with the builders or the land purchase. I was soon to be the owner of a piece of property with enough clay on it to make about five billion hand-thrown pots! Finally, our real estate agent called in a lawyer who basically told us that there was no way that we were going to come out of this deal well if it went to court. His opinion was that we should just buy the land and be done with it. We could have done just that, and survived financially, but we didn't want to be forced to buy land that we really had no use for. Our real estate agent, sensing our angst, said "Let's try to get out of this deal one more time." We sent a contract to the seller dissolving the agreement, hoping that he would sign it.

Lo and behold, the contract came back with the seller's signature! He had completely changed his mind. This was good news! We weren't going to get sued! The house builders refunded our down payment money! Even better news! And I allowed the potential buyer for the business to back out because things just didn't feel right. They were still going to rent the house, so that worry was taken care of. Shortly after all this, the business secured an account that brought in eighty percent more money per month than the business had ever made before. I ended up having to hire even more staff. So God took care of that too.

God's Plans Look Different

There was one main lesson that I learned from this whole experience. It was this: "God's plans very rarely look like our plans—but God's plans are always better." The way Pam and I had strategized it, we would have been living on six acres of land with one tree, a huge mortgage, and a job that I wouldn't have been happy with. The way that God planned it, we had a house on 20 acres of prime land, a reasonable mortgage, renters to build equity in an extra house, and a revitalized business that was making more money than ever before.

I don't know why we get so caught up in our own schemes. I don't know about you, but when I get a direction or an idea in my head, I pursue it with a dogged determination. I'm like a pit bull with a sixteen-ounce sirloin. I just won't let go.

The problem is that I change the plan, I re-form it to fit into the shape that I think it should be. And most disturbingly, I try to make it come true through my own power. I will surge forward, no matter if it is advisable or not. So, what starts out as God's plan, quickly becomes "Ben's scheme loosely based on God's plan." God's direction turns into a footnote on the bottom of the final page. I know that you never do this, but I do.

Here's the rub; God knows a lot better than we do. I think we tend to forget that at times, but hey, there's no shame in admitting it, after all, this is the person that created the flow of time, it stands to reason that He may know a few things that we don't.

Sometimes I picture God up in heaven like a mother who has just cleaned the house only to have their lovely child come in covered with mud. I can just see Him up there, saying "What in the world are you doing? I just cleaned this up! Now you're tracking mud all over my clean floor!" I'm sure if this vision is just a product of my overactive imagination, but it's kind of fun anyway, don't you think?

The thing that I am learning is that I have to trust that God's plan is better than mine, and I need to wait while He accomplishes His purpose. Jeremiah 29:11 says "I know what I'm doing. I have it all planned out— plans to take care of you, not abandon you, plans to give you the future you hope for." (MSG) Habakkuk 2: 3 says: "For the revelation awaits an appointed time; it speaks of the end and will not prove false. Though it linger, wait for it; it will certainly come and will not delay." (NIV) When

God puts a plan in motion, He will fulfill it. Period. It doesn't matter what we see in the natural world, He will prove true.

Some of you, like me, are tempted to run ahead of God's plan. You want more than anything to move as quickly as possible and will do whatever it takes to accomplish the objective in an expedient manner—don't. Some of you are tempted to lag behind God's strategy. You are so afraid of taking the wrong step, that you don't take a step at all—don't.

God's plan is perfect. As it says in Habakkuk, His strategy moves at its own pace. It moves at the only speed that it can to fulfill its purpose. It is very much in our best interest to move forward at the velocity that the plan dictates.

Remember, God knows more than us—"I make known the end from the beginning, from ancient times, what is still to come." (Isaiah 46:10 NIV) and so His plans look a lot different than ours. They move at a different pace, they accomplish different purposes than we think they will. There is one thing that we can know with certainty when it comes to His blueprints, though. They are always better than ours.

I am the type of person that plans ahead. Like many of you, I am a problem solver. I am working hard not to let that personality trait mess up the plans that God has for me. The Bible says: "Be still and know that I am God." (Ps. 46:10 NIV) I am trying to live that... it is a long road. And I still don't get to wear a beret and read poetry on the weekends!

The Valley of Lost Keys

Winter in Michigan is 14 months long. At least that is what it seems like. In order to fight the incredible boredom and take arms against the onslaught of snow-driven depression, the inhabitants of this cold state participate in snow sports. Or sit inside and watch HBO. Actually, I think a larger number of us partake of the latter than the former, but in any event, there are those that pretend to like the cold temperatures, the Arctic winds and the frozen precipitation that blankets everything by trying to do something outside.

What type of things can you do in the snow, you ask? Well, I'm glad you brought that up. You can, um, get frostbite, catch a cold, freeze… What? That's not the type of thing that you were looking for? OK. Fine. I will tell you of the snowy pastimes.

There is snowmobiling. Basically, sitting on top of a jet engine and going over 80 miles per hour through the trees, the whole time listening to the engine whine like a supersonic mosquito. Some people enjoy skiing or snowboarding. This consists of strapping either one or two boards on the bottom of your feet and trying to run over those who are fortunate enough to have fallen already on the way down. There is ice fishing, which interestingly enough is not fishing for ice (otherwise I think I would be much better at it).

These activities begin a list which include: snowshoeing, cross-country skiing, bobsledding, figure skating, sledding, building snow forts, having snowball fights, trying to start your car and snow juniping.

I can picture about half of you reading this scratching your heads and thinking; "I've never heard of snow juniping." The other half of you just skipped over that part and are now going back and the wonderment is just starting. A couple of you even read it wrong and instead of seeing "snow juniping," you saw the words "snow jumping" which brought to mind pictures of jumping from a rooftop into large snow drift. And as fun as that sounds, it is not snow juniping. There is a very good reason that you have never heard of snow juniping. It is because I invented it. (Patent pending, all rights reserved, copyright held by me.)

Winter is long. There are times when you must break out and express yourself. Where something inside screams to let go with the rapture of being alive and loose the furry beast of fun. You reach a point when you realize that if you don't give into this feeling, innocent passers-by may suffer as you pelt them with bologna for no apparent reason. It was in this spirit and for this purpose that snow juniping was born.

After three months of winter, each sunset coming before five o'clock, each day seeming only twenty minutes long, and glimpses of the sun more precious than platinum, I was tired of it. Actually, that's a huge understatement! I was fed up, put out, closed-in and boiling over!

As a friend and I were walking back to my dorm one night, I yelled like a rebel storming the Death Star and began to dance, skip, hop, run, twirl and roll in the snow. I cavorted with wild abandon, flailing around like a man emancipated from death row—oblivious to all but the bliss of expression. I didn't care that there were people sticking their heads out of their dorm windows and yelling at me to shut up, I was enraptured in the moment. I think my friend felt sorry for me and joined in. (Obviously, he wasn't as good as I was, though.)

There, in the dead of winter, in the middle of Michigan, snow juniping was born. The clinical definition of snow juniping is: "To throw off the shackles of winter blackness and celebrate without restraint the spark of life, no matter how faint, to reach for hope of spring with no thought to how far off it seems. This activity includes gyrations, dances and vocalizations wholly spontaneous and not imitative of anything hitherto existing." (Definition provided by "The Eggers Exhaustive Unabridged Dictionary of Imaginary Words" pub. 1493)

Please understand: snow juniping is NOT cavorting in the snow. By definition, snow juniping is without restraint and consists of movements and sounds that have never been heard before. Anyway, now that we have the definition out of the way, let us proceed with the story.

About fifteen minutes later, I fell to my back in exhaustion, breathing out steam and looking with wonder at the stars that seemed to brighten with the joy of our expression. Elated and worn out by our snow juniping, my friend and I continued on our way to our dorm rooms. When I reached mine, however, I found that I could not enter. I had lost my keys. I know, it seems like I lose my keys a lot.

Well, of course I knew where they were. I had lost them during my snow juniping. When I write the official Snow Juniping Guide, that will have to be one of the advisories for Chapter Seven—"When snow juniping, make sure that keys and other pocket articles are secured with an official snow juniping-designated observer in order to minimize the risk of serious injury or loss of personal property. The S.J.L.A. (Snow Juniping League of America) assumes no responsibility for items that are lost as a result of failing to properly secure said items."

So I went back out into thirty degree below zero weather to look for my keys. My eyes fell on the official snow juniping field and my heart sank. There was an area about fifty meters wide by seventy-five meters long with two feet of snow that had been pockmarked with shoe prints. As I looked at what seemed like an acre of churned up snow, I knew that the chances of finding my keys were about as slim as finding the snow that I had just juniped through in a very hot place.

Nevertheless, I looked. And I searched. I examined the ground with single-minded determination and a magnifying glass. I even crawled around on my hands and knees in a desperate attempt to locate the missing keys—all to no avail.

Two hours later, freezing, frostbitten, and thinking that the disadvantages of snow juniping far outweighed the benefits, I trudged indoors. I located my resident advisor who opened my door for me while informing me that the cost to change the lock on the door was going to be thirty-five dollars.

I didn't have thirty-five dollars. I didn't even have one dollar. I worked two jobs on campus just to pay for my schooling. I drank strange concoctions that my friends made with the leftovers from their plates to earn extra cash. I ate my roommate's pizza crusts because I didn't have enough money to buy my own. (Pizza, not pizza crusts.) I was a destitute college student. Now I know you didn't do any weird things like that, but don't judge me, I got through college with very little debt. It seems there is a shortage of people that will drink things with leftover pizza, salt, ketchup, mustard and pop in it. So those dares paid pretty well.

Burdened with this knowledge and utterly defeated, I climbed onto my bunk and went to bed. As I lay there, inches from the asbestos tile, I began to pray. I told the Lord about my unfortunate financial situation. I told the Lord I didn't have enough money to pay for a change in my lock. And after that, I told the Lord that I didn't have enough money to pay for a lock change—again, even though He already knew. I just wanted to make sure that He understood the gravity of the situation.

As I was lying there, I felt the Lord speak to my heart. It was a feeling that I got in the pit of my stomach. And that feeling said "Wait three days."

God's directions don't always make a lot of sense. I spent the next half hour arguing with myself over whether or not it was really God that put that in my spirit, but I knew it was. It just didn't line up with any logic. It was the middle of winter. We were only in the third month of a six month winter. It was thirty degrees below zero and getting colder. My friend and I had been over that patch of ground so many times, they were thinking of naming the field in our honor. There was snow all over the ground. And did I mention it was cold outside?!

Every ounce of logic inside me said that I should just call my parents and have them send me some money so I could get the lock changed, but there was a small bit of me that wanted to see what God was going to do. So I waited.

Somehow, I convinced my roommate to take his key off his key ring, tie a string around it and leave it under the door so that we could pull it out and use it to unlock the lock. Yes, yes, I know it wasn't safe and secure. What do you want from me, I was a college student! I'm not sure what my roommate's willingness to participate in this hair-brained plan says about his character, but I will let you draw your own conclusions.

For three days this continued. The weather stayed the same, and it even got a bit colder. My roommate's patience was wearing thin about our key arrangement. Every time I went by the snow juniping field, I searched for the keys, but never found them. I started to think, *What in the world am I doing?*

The third day dawned like any other. I pulled myself out of bed and started to go into the bathroom to get ready for the day when a curious sound caught my attention. I peered out the window when what to my wondering eyes should appear? Drops of water. There was water falling from the roof! The snow was melting! I looked at the temperature gauge and it read sixty-one degrees! It was sixty-one degrees in February! I was so excited, I put on any clothes I could find! I called my friend, met him at the field, and immediately felt embarrassed by my poor choice of clothing. Apparently, wearing your roommate's girlfriend's nightgown isn't the best option.

No matter; now was not the time for embarrassment. Now was the time for finding keys! I began to search at one side of the field, he started at the other. The snow had melted and the ground was covered with mud and mashed grass. I began walking across the area in question when my friend called to me. He said "Ben, what color were your keys?" I answered back: "Key colored!" He said, "Is this them?" Upon which he held his hand up and lo and behold, there, dangling from his fingers were my keys!

Angels did not appear and start singing the "Hallelujah Chorus," but it was as close as it could get in my mind! I abandoned all decorum and started snow juniping. After making sure my pockets were empty.

Listening to God

God wants to speak to us. Prayer is a conversation with God. Many times we have the talking part down pretty well. "God, I pray that you would bless me… I need… Please be with…" But that's a one-sided conversation. Think about times when you get together with your friends. You never do all the talking, do you? Why not? Because conversation is never as satisfying when you talk all the time. That was what I tended to do with God—talk but not listen.

I think somehow, we've forgotten that our conversations with God should be two-sided. So many times we want to fill up the silence with sound—whether it is telling God what our requests are or worship music, or even television. Unfortunately, when we do that, we can't hear His still, small voice.

As I was lying there in bed listening, God spoke. He said, "Wait three days." Now I didn't hear God speak audibly, and I didn't see a white light or anything like that. There was no thunderclap with the voice like the sound of rushing waters. It was nothing like what you would see in the movies.

The actual process was very simple. I prayed and told God the situation, I told Him my concerns, and I asked for Him to provide. Then I listened. In silence. All of a sudden I had the idea come into my head that I was supposed to wait three days.

I can hear some of you say, "That wasn't God, that was just your mind coming up with that thought." The Bible says "When you come looking for Me, you'll find Me." (Jer. 29:13 MSG) God does not want a one-sided relationship with us, and yes He speaks to us through the Bible and through other people, but sometimes He wants to speak directly to the situations in our individual lives.

Did I know for sure that God spoke to me? No. That is where faith comes in. In Hebrews it talks about faith and says that, "Faith is being sure of what we hope for and certain of what we do not see." (Heb. 11:1 NIV) When I felt God speak to my heart, I took a step of faith. I could have been wrong, but against logic, I obeyed God. I chose to trust Him. I chose to trust my ability to hear His voice. I chose to believe.

Knowing if it is God speaking comes in stages. If you feel God telling you to jump off a building to show that you are a great Christian, don't. The Bible says "…His sheep follow Him because they know His voice." (Joh. 10:4 NIV) I have found that in my life, God didn't start speaking to my heart by asking me to quit my job, sell my house for a pair of sandals and move to California to subsist on cacti and grass. He started with small things—like, "That wasn't a very nice thing to say, you should go and apologize." The more you listen in small things, the more you have faith to obey in larger things.

It says in Matthew 25:21, "Well done, good and faithful servant! You have been faithful with a few things; I will put you in charge of many things. Come and share your master's happiness!" (NIV) There is a progression here. As we listen to God's voice and then obey in smaller things, then the next time we become more confident in hearing His voice. We begin to know Him and trust that the things that He asks us to do will help us. He knows what it takes to build the trust relationship with us.

One thing to keep in mind is that God never asks us to do something that goes against what He commands in the Bible. This is an important caveat, because sometimes someone will come up to me and say, "I feel like God's telling me to divorce my wife." I say ,"Oh really." They say, "Yup, and after that, I'm supposed to cover myself in mud and sacrifice a goat." I say, "Are you sure you're not spelling God S-a-t-a-n?" God does not contradict Himself. Check out what the Bible says, and when it is God telling you something, the Bible will just confirm what He is saying.

The final thing about listening to God is that you need to take it to the next step. Obedience. Notice that the verse above says, "My sheep know my voice and they follow me." They follow me. It does me no good to hear the wonderful things that God has for my life, that He wants for me and then do nothing. I have to obey. That is where we get stuck so many times. We doubt what God is saying—or more to the point, we doubt our ability to hear God. Or we start to look at what God is asking of us in the light of what is logical—and it doesn't make sense. And the more we reason out what He has asked us to do and compare it to conventional wisdom, the more it keeps us from acting on it—the more we doubt, and we are frozen in inaction.

If I would not have obeyed God in the "Snow Juniping Incident," I would have been out thirty-five dollars, and worse, I would have missed seeing the great thing that God wanted to do in my life. It wouldn't have built my faith, it wouldn't have shown me how much God cared for me, it wouldn't have taught me about listening to God. Don't be frozen by inaction! If you make a mistake, there is grace. If it is truly God's voice and He is asking you to do something big, He will usually confirm it several ways.

The important thing is that we have to get off of our sofa-beds and do something. We have to move forward. If you look at Newton's laws of motion, you find that it takes much less force to redirect something that is already in motion than it takes to start something moving from a dead stop. I encourage you to get in motion. Make mistakes, it's OK! Listen to God's voice. Let Him challenge you in your faith.

God speaks to us and when we listen and then obey, He has great things that He wants to bring to pass in our lives. That really fires me up! Think about it; the one that placed the stars in motion has me on His mind! And not only does He want good things for me, He has the power to make them happen! Now, if I could only hear Him say that He wants me to buy a yacht...

All Work and No Pay

I went to college for Visual Communication. I thought I was going to art school to become a fine artist—to paint, sculpt, live in a flat with a skateboarding half-pipe, and sport a ponytail. Not so. I was going to school to become a graphic designer. No ponytail, no painting, I had to trade in my idyllic vision for a shirt and tie, stress and extreme deadlines. I guess I didn't do my research very well if I didn't know what I was going into. Or maybe I'm just not too bright, but the jury is still out on that one. I know, you are still scratching your head trying to figure out what visual communication is. Believe me, when I got into college, I was too.

Simply put, a graphic designer is a person that visually lays out advertisements, posters, brochures, annual reports, and other marketing materials. They decide what an ad should look like, or what picture should go on a poster. I know this sounds like an easy process, and you are thinking, "Hey, I can do the same thing at home." It's true, you can, but there is a lot of training that goes into being a graphic designer.

To be a good designer, you must be able to communicate feelings and vision to a specific audience. This requires empathy with an audience that may be much different than who you are—like "motorcycle gangs." You have to understand what that group thinks, what motivates them and then use images and words that communicate to that group. Actually, right now, communicating to any group seems to take the form of putting a scantily clad woman on the cover holding the product. But I digress.

Because you need to understand and communicate with such a wide variety of audiences, there were classes on the psychology of color, typography, photo manipulation, design, web programming, art history and other equally numbing classes.

The madcap world of advertising is a deadline driven business. At any one time, a graphic designer may have between fifteen and twenty different projects going. Each of these will have its own deadlines. Each will have its own pitfalls, disasters and triumphs.

Our professors had worked in the design world for many years. They were very good and so they pushed us. Hard. We would have between thirty and forty hours of homework to do each week. At night. That was on a week that there wasn't a deadline looming. One girl was especially notorious for pushing herself to the limit. On a deadline week, each morning we would ask her a question. The question was: "How long has it been now?" She would say, "fifty-seven hours." This would tell us how long she had been awake. The number probably told us how long she had gone without showering as well, but we didn't delve too deeply into that subject.

Our professors did prepare us. We would bring in the projects that we had stayed up for days working on. We would stand in front of the class and tell the reasons we did different things—why we used a certain typeface, or what a color might mean to the target market. They would look at us with fishy, cold blue eyes and tell us that the idea sucked. It was an incredibly empowering and joyous experience, you should try it sometime!

I found out later that they were actually doing us a favor. You see, in the design world, many times you will have to stand up in front of a board of directors, many who make more in a day that you make all year, and explain why the idea that you worked so hard on is valid. And yes, sometimes they don't like it. It was invaluable learning how to handle that situation. Of course, we didn't really understand that while we were having our dreams torn apart brick-by-brick. But, as the old saying goes, whatever doesn't kill you makes you stronger—or causes you to lose your hair.

For some odd reason, I thrived on the pressure and stress of the design world, and after college, instead of going to work for a company somewhere, I started my own design firm. Actually, I started freelancing from the back bedroom of our home, but that's the same, isn't it?

Fast forward ten years. I had been in business for myself since college and had shed some of the stupid mistakes that I made at first. Not as many as I would have hoped for, but I was getting better. The business was thriving, we were doing well over six figures in revenue and I had seven employees. We did projects for a lot of different clients, but we had one client that comprised about sixty-five percent of our business.

We had worked with this client for about two years and did almost all of their marketing and design. This enabled us to be involved with a wide variety of projects ranging from logo and identity concepts to signage. We went on photo shoots to different locations and were able to determine their marketing direction. It was great.

Everything was going well when I got a call from the client. They had had a budget meeting and couldn't afford us anymore. They were going to bring their marketing in-house and were terminating our contract in one month.

I have heard it said that it's not what happens to a person, but how they react to it that tells you what's on the inside. Well, I wanted to scream and cry like a little baby, so I'm not sure what was on the inside of me. I didn't scream and cry, though, because I knew it would do no good. I had employees that needed me and I had to come up with a plan to move ahead or give up.

As I thought and prayed about the situation, I knew that giving up wasn't an option. So I started to run some numbers. I cut it down to the bare essentials. No more free soft drinks. Nothing but the bare essentials. Instead of toilet paper, we would use the paper from the many credit card applications we received. Just kidding! We would operate on bare bones until we could build up the client base again. That way, at least we could keep the doors open.

It was a good plan with only two down sides. The first was that I had to lay someone off. The company that no longer required our services needed someone to do the work that we used to do for them, though, so I was able to find that employee a job. Problem solved. The second problem was a little harder. I had to lay myself off. In truth, I couldn't be laid off, so I just had to work without pay for an indefinite period of time. Until things got better or the world exploded in fire and brimstone— whichever came sooner. Sometimes I thought that the latter would happen before the first with the way things were going!

I was unemployed. I had the stress of a business that was on the verge of insolvency. I had employees depending on me to bring in new business so that they could keep their jobs. I was making no money. And I couldn't find another job, because I had to work fifty to sixty hours a week. This had to be one of the worst promotions that I had ever had!

And just when things looked like they couldn't get any worse, they did. About three months after we lost the account, the inevitable occurred. We found ourselves without enough business. All of the jobs had just dried up. We were still cutting back and were running as lean as we could but it wasn't enough. Our inflows didn't even come close to our outflows! I thought; *Well, what about next month?* No dice. As I looked over the next few months, I came face-to-face with a sad fact. We simply weren't going to make it as a business unless we did something drastic.

I knew that we could not continue to go into the red with the business, so after talking it over with Pam, we committed (again) to keeping the business going and began to loan the business money. Believe me, I had prayed countless times telling God that I was more than willing to give up the business, sell it, auction it off, walk away from it or just give it to the next person that walked through the door. But I guess I hadn't suffered enough, He wanted me to stick it out. The cash reserves that the business had built up had been depleted purchasing new office space, so we dipped into our own meager savings to keep the business going. This went on month after month after month.

As we reached the bottom of our means monetarily, physically, and emotionally, we noticed something peculiar. God was meeting our needs. It had been about nine months since I had begun to work without pay. We had loaned the business over $30,000. Our savings account was non-existent. We sold our mutual funds, both personal and business. We cashed out our retirement account. There was no money for emergencies or anything else—but we were making it.

Pam and I realized that no matter what bills came up, just at the right time, God brought in some funds to cover the bill. I would do the bills, paying our tithe to God first, and then pray, because there wasn't enough to pay all of them. I would put the rest of the bills in God's hands and trust Him to take care of it. You know what? He always did. We had reached the end of our resources and had been brought to the point that we had to depend entirely on God because there was no way in the normal order of the universe that we would be able to pay our bills, let alone afford luxuries like food and water!

Time after time, something miraculous happened to meet our needs. Sometimes it was a neighbor bringing over dinner, or watching our kids for free so that Pam and I could go out on a date. Several times a check that we didn't anticipate showed up at our door. And for Christmas, we had planned for a low-key celebration—no presents, a tree cut from our own land, and some special time with our kids. Our extended family, however, found out about it and sent us money to buy the children Christmas presents!

It wasn't that we wouldn't have had a wonderful Christmas without presents, but God wanted to provide more that we could have imagined. Through that one, simple act, God showed us more love and helped us to understand more of His greatness than if doves would have dropped out of heaven singing the "Hallelujah Chorus."

That's when it hit me. We were learning a lesson through this trial. As Pam and I looked back over our married life, we had always trusted in our ability to generate income. It was never a problem. Pam had a great job, and I had built a successful company. We had thousands in the bank and never REALLY trusted God to provide for us. We trusted our ability to earn money. Big difference!

God allowed all of the trust we had in our abilities to be wiped out. Demolished. Then, just to be on the safe side, crushed. We had nothing else to lean on. We had to trust in God. There was no one else. And He provided. Each and every week. Every single bill was paid. Sometimes they were a few days late, but they got paid. And we came to a deeper place of trust in our relationship with God.

It was a back-breaking, exhausting, difficult lesson! I wish I wasn't so thick-headed so that I could have learned it in an easier manner, but looking back, I wouldn't trade that knowledge for anything. I wouldn't trade the depth of my trust for an easier road. I would choose to walk that way again, because the worst that could ever happen is that all the other insubstantial possessions would be stripped away and I would be left with the one thing I needed in the first place. God.

I would like to say that after we came to the realization that we needed to lean on God for our provision, things immediately got better and we had money galore, but that just isn't true. I ended up being without a paycheck for a full year and a half. I guess God really wanted to make sure that I had learned what I needed to learn. I'd like to think I did—because as much as I am thankful for the lessons I learned, I really, really don't want to go through that again.

Faith

Faith is something that we can only acquire through experience. You cannot be taught faith through higher learning, studying, or through vicarious observation. It must be ingested whole. It must be taken into your system and allowed to become part of who you are.

Faith is like marathon training. When you train for a marathon, you rarely run over thirteen miles (half the distance of the final race). Your normal weekday runs are between five and eight miles. On the weekend, you will do longer runs, but most of the time it is twenty miles or less. You never run the full twenty-six point two miles of a full marathon. So there is an air of uncertainty about it. When it comes down to the race, there is an element in your brain that says; "I've never actually run this far before. I've come somewhat close, but this is six miles farther than I've ever run in my training." Then you think about all those stories that you have heard before—about people losing control of their bodies after twenty miles, about people collapsing and almost dying trying to finish this abnormally long race. And there comes a time when you have to choose to put all of those things behind you, forget about them and believe beyond what you know. You have to trust your training and put your foot out and start running.

Running a marathon is going as far as you can in training, and then reaching out and going farther. It pushes your body and your mind past their limits. That's the way it is with faith. You come up to the edge of what you know. You draw on all your past experiences, you try to glean knowledge from others who have been in similar situations, but quite simply, you come to the edge of yourself, your abilities, what you can do. And when you are there, God says, "Now step forward."

This is where you have a choice. You won't be able to see what that step holds or what it may mean because you have never been there before. This is uncharted territory. Hebrews puts it this way: "Faith is being sure of what we hope for and certain of what we do not see." (Heb. 11:1 NIV) How can you be certain of the things you cannot see? That's where trust comes in.

To truly push forward in faith, we have to trust in God's faithfulness. If we don't, we will never take that first step. We will never achieve the things God wants for our lives, because we will come up to the edge of what we can do and we will shrink back. How come that isn't good enough to be called faith? Because God always calls us to do much more than we can achieve on our own. It's His way of drawing us closer to Him—of building our trust relationship with Him.

If given a choice, I will choose the easiest path. That seems logical, right? Unfortunately, that's not how faith grows. God is faithful. He is able to provide for you in ways that you cannot imagine. He wants to prove that to you. The price of knowing this faithfulness, though, is going through some extreme conditions. Just like you never know how warm a coat really is until you are in sub-zero weather. That's when it proves its effectiveness. Faith is only faith when you don't know the route and you're way beyond your own abilities.

If I would not have gone through eighteen months of not getting paid, I would not have realized how deep and wide God's faithfulness was. If I still had my savings accounts, my mutual funds, and even my retirement account, I would not have understood how complete and imaginative God's ways of providing are. God had to pare me down to nothing. He had to show me that I can trust in Him and Him alone. My own ability to make money is pitiful next to His extravagant abundance!

"Trust in the Lord with all your heart and lean not on your own understanding. In all your ways acknowledge Him and He will make your paths straight." (Pr. 3:5-6 NIV) We all know this verse, but have you really thought about how much it may cost you to "trust in God with all your heart," and to "acknowledge Him in ALL your ways?" The promise is there—He will make your paths straight, but oftentimes I'm unwilling to pay the true price. I mean who, in their right mind would consciously want things to get bad so that they could build their faith?

Just remember, "We continue to shout our praise even when we're hemmed in with troubles, because we know how troubles can develop passionate patience in us, and how that patience in turn forges the tempered steel of virtue, keeping us alert for whatever God will do next." (Rom. 5:3-4 MSG) You see, God's faithfulness is at its best when we are at the end of the things that we trust in. The eminence of His unswerving devotion is only proved when we throw ourselves into the great unknown of His plan with complete abandon—frigid with fears, timid with hope and uncertain of the outcome.

God has a plan for us, He is faithful. Faith comes when we can look at the future and truly say, "Come what may, I WILL follow you. I don't understand why you have chosen this road, but I trust in Your faithfulness enough that I will step forward. Just one step. I will put out my foot and with all the force of my weight behind it, I will trust that You will be there."

The Incredible Exploding House

The sound of an eruption is never as deafening as the silence in the moments that follow. Let me start at the beginning.

Our graphic design business had outgrown the basement that we were currently using. We sold the house and looked for another place for the business to reside. After searching for quite a while, we found a perfect place. It was located in the heart of the downtown area, two blocks from the main street. When I say main street, I know that you are asking yourself, "Exactly how small is this town?" Well, to answer your question, it's not big enough to have a mall and large enough that you can't throw a rock and hit the other side. I know, some of you are asking, "How big a rock?" and others are saying, "I'll bet I could throw a rock over those mountains." OK, OK, I'll clarify.

Big Rapids, Michigan is a great town. It is about 10,000 people in the summer, and twice that during the school year. It is home to Ferris State University—"Go Bulldogs," and the school adds population, culture, art, fast food restaurants and drunken bashes in which couches get thrown from second story windows. You know, everything you need to foster a fine upstanding Christian community!

The house that we found was six blocks from the university, and was built in 1900. It was a beautiful, stately manor with incredible potential. Notice that I said "incredible potential." For those of you that are well versed in the art of "do-it-yourself," that means that it was a mess. It had wonderful hardwood floors—underneath lime-green carpeting. It had beautiful woodwork—but you hardly noticed it next to the wallpaper that was falling off the walls. The ceilings were nine and a half feet tall (in the places that the plaster wasn't hanging down). Altogether, it had great possibilities—for a lot of backaches!

I was young and optimistic (spelled "d-u-m-b") though, and was up to the task. I called a builder friend, and we got to work. We decided to renovate the house and keep as much of the natural charm and original wood as possible. We knocked out walls, redid plumbing, and ran over a mile of wiring in the downstairs alone. Actually, my builder did many of these things with my help usually consisting of hitting myself multiple times with a hammer. Hey, don't knock it, comic relief is very important on the job site!

We were making great progress. At least I thought we were, it was kind of hard to tell because of the mess everywhere. Plaster and lathe were all over the floor. Wallpaper pieces fell like confetti for no apparent reason. Electrical wiring poked out of outlets like small snakes ready to bite anyone that touched them. We had knocked out a supporting wall and had installed a header instead. I had worked with the builder and another friend on that project, and it was a wonder that no one died as the beam suddenly pushed loose and clouted one of them off his ladder.

This builder had plenty of guts. He told me in detail how he had been electrocuted by 110v, 220v, and 440v electricity—yet he still wired things without turning off the circuit breakers! Yes, the builder certainly did not lack guts. Common sense though, well, I'll let you make the call on that.

It was the day after we put up the header. I got into the building at about ten in the morning and went upstairs to our temporary offices. On the way in I had smelled gas though, so I went downstairs and talked to the person who was helping the builder. He didn't notice it, but said when the builder got back from running errands, he would check with him.

I didn't think anything more of it and went upstairs. We had set up temporary office space in one of the bedrooms while the downstairs was refurbished. I began to work. There were three of us in the office that day and we were working on several different projects. I was particularly engrossed in a design question with one of the designers when something arrested my attention.

You've seen those movies where an entire planet explodes, right? It starts small. You see a gout of flame. Silently, it spreads, building in intensity, then the camera pulls back and the entire planet erupts in flame. Then, after a moment, the sound comes. It starts as a low rumble, and explodes into a cacophony of sound that vibrates you to your toes. This is what we experienced in the little fifteen-by-seventeen foot room we were using as an office. Except a planet didn't explode.

Everything else happened exactly like the movies, though. First, we felt the entire floor lift up as the house jumped off the foundation. Then came the boom. It rattled the windows and made us all look at each other with wide eyes wondering if we would next see aliens descend from the heavens on a green beam of light demanding to speak to our leader.

Slowly, reason returned to me and I knew what the cause of the sound was. Something must have fallen over downstairs—like an entire wall! No, wait, I would run downstairs and find out that the header that we had just put in had collapsed and crushed one of the builders! In any event, I tore out of the office and rushed down the stairs, fully expecting to need an ambulance and have to make a very difficult call to the next of kin. I rounded the banister and a curious sight met my eyes. Smoke was pouring out of the vents!

This was puzzling. I looked through the haze, but didn't find anyone—impaled, crushed or otherwise broken, so I continued onward. I pushed through the normal debris all over the floor, frantically searching each and every room, afraid of what I would find.

With each step, I grew more apprehensive as I approached the basement. This house was built before block or poured foundations. It was made out of stones. Yes, just regular rocks that you would find in your back yard. In places, there were strange nooks and crannies (I think they were for hiding drugs,) and it was the type of place where a human skeleton chained to the wall wouldn't seem out of place! Morally repugnant, yes, out of place, no. Then there was the furnace.

I'm sure you've heard of an octopus furnace. It's called that because it looks like, well, an octopus. There is a big oven-type structure with ductwork that comes out of the top at all sorts of crazy angles. People would shovel coal into the oven area and it would heat the house. This one had been converted to use gas, but it was the biggest I had ever seen. It was about seven feet in diameter and eight feet tall. More than enough room to roast a human. So you can understand the reasons for my apprehension about the basement.

But as I opened the basement door, my anxiety turned to relief and puzzlement. The builder and his helper came out of the basement door completely gray. They looked as if they had been coated in talcum powder! I wasn't sure if they were auditioning for a part in a weird off-Broadway musical or just trying their hand at Kabuki Theater! One good thing that I realized as I gazed upon them, though, was that they seemed to be whole and hale with all limbs attached in the approximate places as they should be.

Actually, they were downright giddy! They were stumbling and laughing (when they weren't coughing). I started to wonder if the stuff that was covering them had some "medicinal purposes!" Slowly, the wonder and relief of finding them in a healthy state was replaced by something else. Indignation.

"What in the world happened?!" I asked. The tale that I heard then was beyond anything that I could have dreamed up, both because of its lack of common sense and because of my builder's sheer audacity.

As we were working on the wiring, one of things that I had requested was that the heating control system would be replaced with a thermostat that was assembled after 1950. This would decrease the amount of gas usage in a system that was already only about three percent efficient. This change was going to increase the furnace efficiency by a whopping one percent if I was lucky. Yea! So the old thermostat was disconnected and the new thermostat was installed. The problem was, during the electrical rewiring the day before, the pilot had gone out in the giant octopus furnace in the basement.

There was no automatic shutdown on the furnace, and the gas detectors hadn't been installed yet, so the result was that for the entire night, gas poured out of the heating vents into the house! That was what I had smelled that morning when I came in to work. I shudder to think what would have happened if we hadn't caught the problem in time. For the whole morning, four people, including myself were working in a house filled with gas! We could have gone to sleep and woken up lying on a cloud!

My builder found the problem and decided to save me some time. This is where it gets interesting. You see, if you discover a gas leak and call the gas company, they will come out, cordon off the area and evacuate everyone in the surrounding area, usually an entire block or more. They will then dissipate the gas in a safe and calm manner. Unfortunately, this process usually takes most of the day and so we would have lost a whole day of work. My builder knew this and decided that he would be a nice guy and try to make it so that we could take care of the problem in a much quicker—albeit less safe manner.

You remember that I had mentioned that my builder had plenty of guts, but the common sense area was a little more up for grabs? This is a case in point. With his Carhartt jacket pulled up over his head for protection, he thought it would be a good idea to light a match! This would ignite the excess gas and make the air safe to breathe. Sounds like a good idea, right? I don't recommend it. He expected a blast as he held the lighter toward the furnace, but he was unprepared for the twenty-five foot gout of flame that shot out of the furnace access and enveloped him in a supernova!

The explosion ran through the entire house's duct system, pushing dirt and soot in front of the expanding cloud and out of the vents, sending a mushroom cloud spewing ten feet into the air to fall down like the ash from a volcano, covering everything, living and dead. This is what I mistook for smoke as I came tearing down the stairs in my mad dash to try to determine what had happened. The expansion of the gas as it ignited caused the entire house to buckle and jump to the point that it felt like it lifted the house off of its foundation! Whether or not that actually happened is something only God knows for sure.

Incredibly enough, we all emerged from that episode unscathed. Even the builder and his helper were OK. They just had to wash their clothes. Upstairs, we had to dust the entire office, but both of my designers were fine. I, on the other hand, was left with the knowledge that we all could have died that day.

Protection

The abrupt comprehension of your own mortality is a curious thing. You begin to see things in sharp relief. God protected not only me that day, but he protected four other people too. The biggest thing that I learned about God's faithfulness through this experience is that God is extremely constant in protecting us. In the Bible, He says that He will protect us, but this episode really clinched it for me.

I mean, think about all the things that could have gone wrong that day! We could have missed the smell of gas and slowly been killed, or we could have just chalked the gas smell up to our imaginations and the result would have been the same. The explosion could have killed the builder and my friend. The contractor had just gotten engaged, and my friend who was helping him had a wife and four kids. Their lives would have been shattered for all time! The entire house could have moved off its foundation and collapsed! You see, there were so many things that could have gone wrong in this scenario, that it is almost unbelievable that we came out unscathed!

If I would not have come into the house and smelled the gas, we could have all gone to sleep and never woken up. And while the Bible tells us to search for eternal rewards, I'm not ready to claim them yet. There is one reason only that things turned out as well as they did. God's protection. Pure and simple.

Think about the contractor—here he is lighting God only knows how much gas with only his jacket as protection! He didn't even get his eyebrows singed! If that's not a sign of God's protection, I don't know what is!

The Bible says that God would, "...command His angels concerning you, and they will lift you up in their hands, so that you will not strike your foot against a stone." (Mat. 4:6 NIV) There are so many people that go through life and expect bad things to happen to them. They are always looking around the corner anticipating the next car crash, the next sickness, the next financial disaster. I understand, I have been in that place. I didn't trust in God's faithful protection.

Make no mistake, bad things happen. It's not God's fault. But here's the rub. When you are going though a string of seemingly endless bad situations, you have a choice. Yes, that's right, a choice. You can't change the things that happen to you, be it good or bad, but you can choose how you will react to them.

You can choose to believe that the evil that happens to you is just the way life is. That bad things happen for no reason and you are just a leaf that's tossed around by every difficult situation that comes. You can abdicate control of your life to that fickle mistress, fate, and give up. But if you do, you will begin to look for the stormy side of every situation and every time you come across one you will add that to the tally to support your theory that "bad things happen."

Or you can choose to trust in God's faithfulness—His protection. When something bad happens, you can acknowledge that that was a tough situation, but choose to believe in God's faithfulness. You can look for the good in the situation. You can even think about possible things that God was protecting you from in allowing you to go through this!

Sometimes, when I get a flat tire, and I am on the way to an important meeting, instead of wallowing in the frustration of the missed meeting, I will think about what God may have been protecting me from. Maybe it was a car accident, maybe it wasn't a good day for the person I was going to meet with and the meeting would have gone badly, maybe God wanted me to slow down so He could show me something. You see how important trust in God's protection is?

It's your choice, though. You can trust with all your heart that the Bible doesn't lie. When it says that God protects those that love Him, that's what it means. You can choose to believe that it will get better, but you have to make a conscious effort to think that way, it doesn't come naturally.

It is not easy to get out of the negative-thinking spiral when everything seems to go wrong, but it is absolutely necessary! It truly is a "glass half full, glass half empty" thing. The Bible says, speaking of man, "For as he thinks in his heart, so is he." (Pr. 23:7 NKJV) So, what happens when you focus on the negative things that have happened to you, and the circumstances you can't understand in your life? You become negative and you expect your life to be bad. You put yourself in the place of God, expecting to be all-knowing and you find that things get worse.

On the other hand, what happens when you choose to trust in a God that is faithful, in a God that protects you, in a God that knows the end from the beginning? That's what you will find. God protects you. The Bible says it, it's true, end of story! There are no mitigating circumstances. The only difference is whether you believe it or not. Whether you can truly trust that God wants the best for you and will not abandon you when times get tough. That deep belief makes all the difference.

God's protection is always there. It's like the air, it is a force of nature. You can say that it doesn't exist, you can fight with every breath against it, but it doesn't make the air disappear. You are just fighting against something that's main purpose is to help you! Or you can breathe deeply and thank God with every breath! You can trust in the nature of oxygen to provide what you need to keep your body moving.

God's protection is like that. When you choose to breathe deeply and put your trust in it, you are aligning yourself with a force that is there to aid you. You are trusting in the nature of God's protection—that it will do as it's supposed to do—protect you. You are in the place that God has desired for you—even if your whole world erupts (or just your house).

The exploding house episode taught me so much about trusting in God's protection. Actually, when I think about it, it did more than one good thing—it also cleaned out the entire furnace duct work. I hear that you have to pay people good money to do that. What a racket! Who knew all you had to do was let gas leak into your house for a night and light a match? So much easier!

Flip Me Over

It's funny how your entire life can change in one blink of a gnat's eye. (Actually, I'm just assuming that gnats blink, I haven't actually done any exhaustive research on the matter, so if you, the reader, happen to know that gnats in fact do not blink, then I give you leave to alter the first sentence to match something that coincides with nature. See how accommodating I am?) Anyway, when you are caught up in the normal hum-drum of everyday life, you yearn for something to break the monotony. Only you never expect it to happen. Unfortunately, sometimes those experiences slam into your life like a sledgehammer and the results are not what you might have hoped for. God seems to know how to radically change a situation to make things look much different than just a few moments before—even if the reason that you are in that condition is because of your own stupidity.

Pam and I were going through some tough times financially. We had a new child and were trying to run a business and pay all our bills on time. As we looked at our finances, we realized that our expenditures outweighed our income. Now, if you ask an accountant, they will probably call that something like "financial insolvency." To me, that is just a fancy name for "we don't have enough money."

So we looked for ways to cut costs. I was all for putting our child on Ebay and starting the bidding, but for some reason Pam thought that idea was less than perfect. Now before you all start writing me nasty letters telling me what a horrible father I am, here's the disclaimer: "No children were harmed in the making of this book. There was never any thought to sell any of the children, and the anecdote that was just shared was just a cleverly disguised trick to be controversial and thusly sell more books." There, feel better?

We trimmed our budget and bought the thirty-pound bag of Cheetos instead of the smaller bags which saved us a whopping dollar and thirty-nine cents! I know, you're asking; "Why didn't you just cut out Cheetos altogether?" To which I reply; "What's life without Cheetos?" Boy, when you bought this book, I'll bet you didn't expect all of the deep philosophical ponderings that have been discussed at length here did you? Well, consider it a bonus.

Obviously the Cheetos cost-cutting plan was less successful than we had hoped. One actual way to cut costs as we found out, was to trade-in or sell one of our vehicles and buy a less expensive vehicle with cash. We had two cars, both with rather large outstanding loans to the bank. This was not the best decision that we had ever made.

We talked about it. We pondered the situation. We crunched the numbers—and we decided that in order to maximize the effectiveness of our debt reduction plan, we would divest ourselves of our largest debt— our SUV.

This was our favorite car. It said "We've arrived. We have status." It had four-wheel drive and could push through the forty-two inches of Michigan snow like nobody's business. It was more than a vehicle, it was a status symbol. It also guzzled gas like a dehydrated man stumbling into an oasis. Alas, we had to bid it farewell.

I went to a local car dealership and found a car that would suffice. Yes, it was a step down for us and instead of announcing "We've arrived," this car screamed "Here we come!" I reminded myself of our long-term goals, though, and that seemed to dull the ache of giving up our favorite vehicle. So, I made an offer.

This began a long process of offering, counter-offering, talking about options and looking at prices. The salesman went in to discuss the deal with his manager three times! I'm not convinced they weren't talking about the Red Sox instead of my offer but finally, after my five o'clock shadow had turned into two-day stubble, we had an agreement.

We settled on the price of the new car. We arrived on the specific options that would be included. We decided on the delivery date. We agreed that we would trade in our SUV. Then they told me that I owed more on my Explorer than it was worth. Several thousand more. We wouldn't be able to make an even trade. We would have been stuck in the same situation—still in debt, still with a car payment. And to top it off, we would have a car that my grandpa wouldn't drive instead of a sweet SUV! Don't you hate it when that happens?

Well, we couldn't afford to reduce our debt. That sounds strange, I know, but it's the truth. We didn't have enough money for a cheaper car. We were stuck. We got rid of whatever other payments we could, but were still several hundred dollars in the red each month. We weren't sure what to do, so we prayed about the situation, and then just held on for dear life.

To make things even better, the four-wheel drive on the SUV went out! (What's the use of having a four-wheel drive vehicle if only two-wheel drive works?) It had to do with locking hubs or something cool like that, but the long and the short of it was that the four-wheel drive didn't work. Obviously, we couldn't afford to get it fixed, so there we were spending more than we were making, with a vehicle that we couldn't afford to get rid of. Nice, huh?

I mentioned before that God is merciful to us, even when we get into stupid situations ourselves—a fact I am extremely thankful for. My opinion is that when we do get ourselves into situations by our own bad decisions though, He sometimes lets us get out the hard way as His way of cuffing us upside the head and saying, "What in the world were you thinking?" Obviously, my opinion is not backed by weighty theological cross-references, so you can take it or leave it as you see fit. But now that I think about it, maybe that's just the way He helps me.

You see, I was the one that had made the decision to buy the SUV. I was the one that got us into this mess. I was the one that had dug myself into a hole that I couldn't get out of. But then "Dad" (God) had to come to my rescue and bail me out. I have to think that He must have felt a bit like me when I have to extricate one of my children from some stupid situation they have gotten into. I love them more than life itself and would do anything for them—but AAARRRRGGG!

I was on my way to piano lessons. Yes, I took piano lessons as a twenty-something. OK, are you done laughing? I was running late—which I hate. To me, if you're not ten minutes early, you aren't on time. I know, it's incredibly neurotic, but in any event, I was tardy, so I grabbed my keys and rushed out the door, slamming it behind me in my hurry.

My piano teacher lived on a dirt road. And just to satisfy your curiosity, no, there are no cattle roaming the hills next door to her. There are horses, though, so that's good. Anyway, it was about a mile or a little more of gravel road from the highway to her driveway. On either side were fields of some plant that I didn't recognize, bordered by barbed wire fences. Houses dotted either side of the road with ditches deeper than castle moats keeping out the traveling salesmen.

I don't know if you have ever driven on a gravel road, but there is something that is uniquely dangerous about them. Aside from stones flying up and chipping your paint, and breaking your windshield, and dirt coating your entire vehicle, road chatter poses a very real threat. Road chatter is a series of small "speed bumps" that are caused when people accelerate or brake on a gravel road. Your car tires travel over the tops of these bumps and just jump along giving you about as much traction as walking on ice with shoes coated in cooking spray.

Road chatter is not a huge problem for front wheel drive vehicles because all of the power is in the front wheels and it pulls the rest of the car. Unfortunately, it is a different story with rear-wheel drive cars. It is not good for a rear-wheel drive vehicle to accelerate too quickly on a gravel road as I soon found out. I was driving along well above a safe speed, hit some road chatter, and the back end started to slide sideways. I remember thinking: "Well, that's not good." So I adjusted the wheel.

I'm not sure what I expected to happen, but I found out that when you are sliding sideways on a dirt road, at fifty-eight miles per hour, there is not much of a chance that you will be able to pull out of it. Your inertia has pretty much determined your final destination without much involvement from you.

My vehicle went off the road, and hit the ditch. Calling it a ditch doesn't really do it justice, though. It was as wide and deep as an Olympic-sized swimming pool! The vehicle went careening through the air, seemingly independent of gravity, and rode that ditch like a skateboard curling a half-pipe! The vehicle flipped with the greatest of ease and left me suspended from my seatbelt with my head smooshed against the ceiling. A word of advice: "If you want others to think you are cool, try not to do this."

I took a mental assessment of the situation. Question number one: "Can I drive out of this?" Answer: "What are you, dumb?" Question number two: "Why is the roof of the car so close?" Answer: "The impact has cut the amount of cabin space in the vehicle in half by crushing the roof." Question number three: "Why is the motor still running and the radio playing?" Answer: "I don't know, I've just suffered a severe blow to the head!" Thankfully, I have a very thick skull.

I tried the door. It was permanently compressed into the frame and there was no way I could open it. I turned off the engine—because I didn't want to waste gas. Then, I crawled on the ceiling of the vehicle toward the back window, which had been broken out. None of my limbs were broken, but I did have a cut above my eye and blood was dripping on my shoe.

I stumbled across the street, went to the nearest house and rang the doorbell. A boy and his sister answered the door. They were somewhere between the ages of eight and sixteen. I'm not very good at determining age. Hey, give me a break, I had just suffered a hefty blow to my pride! I said, "Can I use your phone, I just crashed?" They looked at me, looked at the smoldering wreck across the street, looked back at me and yelled "Moooooom!" as they tripped over each other in a strenuous attempt have the honor of being the first to bring this amazing tale to her.

Soon a nice lady came to the door and allowed me to use her phone. I called my piano teacher. Hey, it's only polite, I was going to be late for my lesson! Actually, I never got to go to my lesson that day, but instead spent the afternoon talking with a police officer and watching my vehicle be towed. Amazingly, the ambulance didn't need to be called, I was in relatively good health.

A few days later, I saw my vehicle in the junk yard and I was incredulous that I could have walked away from that crash with no more than a small cut on my eyebrow. The windows were broken out and the roof was crushed so that it was almost level with the body of the car. As I went inside to get my CDs out, I realized that glass was everywhere. It was a miracle I wasn't sliced open in my journey from the front to the back.

Well, God truly protected me in the midst of my stupidity. He kept me safe; even though I was driving way too fast—I came out relatively unscathed, when I could have been maimed for life. He protected me from hurting anyone else. Most of all, through that bad circumstance, God rescued me from my abysmal financial situation with the vehicle. Because lo, and behold, a couple of weeks after the crash, our insurance company sent us a check that was large enough to pay off our vehicle—so our financial worries were taken care of as well! Kind of a strange way to bail us out from our own dumb decisions, but there you have it.

God Helps Us In Our Own Stupidity

My car crash experience was one of those times that made me see things with an entirely different perspective. As I gazed at the crushed metal that used to be my vehicle, I couldn't help but think about how quickly life can change. Here I was one minute worrying about finances and life, and how I was late for my piano lesson. The next minute, I could have been paralyzed, or even dead! I truly understood the passage, "Be very careful, then, how you live—not as unwise but as wise, making the most of every opportunity because the days are evil." (Eph. 5:15-16 NIV) You never know, in an instant everything could change.

The biggest thing that I learned through all this though, is that God loves us and cares for us, even when we do stupid things. It was my fault that we were in that financial mess. It was my fault that I was driving too fast and went off the road. But in spite of all that, God still provided a way out! Did He make me go off the road? No way. But He did use the situation that Satan meant for evil and turned it to good.

It all comes back to faithfulness. God is faithful—no matter the reason that you have gotten into your current state of affairs. If I wouldn't have made the financial decision to buy the SUV, we probably wouldn't have been in the debt situation we were in, and we would have had a front-wheel drive car and I probably wouldn't have gone off the road. None of that matters though. God still is faithful, even though I make dumb choices.

It matters more to Him that I try to do what's right, such as trying to draw closer to Him or wanting to know Him, rather than how well I am actually accomplishing the task. I remember what it was like the first time my son played soccer. (I use that term loosely, because it mostly consisted of him standing there and watching the other players run after the ball.) Sometime during the game though, he kicked the ball. Then, he ran after it and kicked it again! I was so proud! He was trying. It didn't matter to me that he wasn't the next Beckam, I was overcome with joy that he was not just standing there picking his nose!

God looks at us the same way. He's so proud of us when we try to please Him, try to get closer to Him, to know Him. The Bible calls David a man after God's own heart. This, after David made some horrid decisions. He chose to sleep with another man's wife. He chose to lie about it. He chose to try to trick the man to cover up his sin! He chose to murder the man! The thing is, though, David also chose to repent.

David realized that he had made mistakes, bad choices, but his true desire was to be close to God—to know Him. That's why the Bible calls David a man after God's own heart. And God was faithful to him. Yes, David paid a horrible price for his choices, but in the midst of his failure, God was faithful.

Realize that God will be faithful no matter what dumb things you do. Turn your heart to Him and draw near to Him. Move forward and know that He has a plan for you. His love for us is greater than we can imagine.

Sometimes we think that when we make bad decisions or mistakes, or outright sin, God's good plans for us go away. We think it's like He's up there thinking, "Wow, look at Ben. I really want to make him prosper. I love him so much. I think I will give him good things in life. Oh, wait, he just spent more than he should have on that electronic gadget! Sorry, guess the plans I have for him are all screwed up, hold the order for good stuff, and serve him a plate of detritus instead."

Do we really want to make God that small? Do we really want a God whose plans can be foiled by something as slight as our bad decisions? God is faithful and His plans are not thwarted. Yes, you have free will, and you CAN choose to walk away from His plans for your life, but if you truly want Him to have sway in your paths, and you are trying your best to follow Him, your dumb choices, bad decisions and even sins cannot stop the good things He has for you!

God knows all of the dumb, sin-filled choices you are going to make. Yet He still made the plans He has for you. It's not about achieving perfection—we can't do that on our own. It's about knowing Him. It's about pursuing a relationship with Him—one where you are fully known and are wanting to fully know Him. He loves you. He protects you. He is faithful in your life. He even rescues you when you are flipping through the air of your own bad decisions.

The strength of My Weakness

Everybody has weaknesses. It is an undeniable fact of life, kind of like the way you can count on every single traffic light being red when you are rushing 120 miles an hour to the hospital with a torn toenail. Of course, I've never done that.

Anyway, weaknesses are just a part of being human. I mean, look, even Superman had a weakness! Now, I'm not sure if an imaginary element counts as a weakness, but the effort was there nonetheless. I truly believe that if the creators of Superman would not have given him a vulnerability, we, as humans would never have come to love him as much as we do. There is something about the fact that he has a weakness that makes him approachable, relatable, human.

Yes, we all have weaknesses. So, the question is—why do we try so hard to hide the very thing that makes us human?

I too have weaknesses. Hang around with me long enough and you will probably come across more of my failures than my strengths. My main flaw though, is that I can't stand having weaknesses! I have a problem with failures in my life. If I have a shortcoming, I will practice and practice until I conquer it. Unfortunately, there are things in our lives that we shouldn't overcome—and that is a lesson that I am still working on learning.

Did you ever wonder why you are the way you are? I amuse myself sometimes by picking out one of my foibles and tracing it back to see if I can find its roots. Actually, it doesn't amuse me as much as frustrate me. I have a streak of perfectionism in me as visible as the white on a skunk. And guess what? Just like so many of the things that affect me now, it sprang from my childhood.

My dad was a pastor. I know some of you just did the "Aaaaahhhhh" of recognition because you are pretty sure that explains a lot. Well, it does, but as with everything, that's not the end of the story.

The church was very demanding on my dad's time and energy. When he would come home, he would be exhausted and escape in the only way that he could. I would come to him with a question, and he would answer; "Mmmmmhmmm," as he stared at a magazine. This was his escape—the way he released the pressure of the never-ending demands of the ministry—those of you who are pastors, you know what I am talking about. I understand it now, but as I was younger, I was just a boy craving his dad's attention.

Many times, when I was in sports, drama, choir, or other activities, my dad wouldn't be there. There was a meeting or he had to work on his sermon, or someone died (as if that's a good excuse!) Suffice to say, my dad would be at my swimming meets if it fit into his schedule. I don't know how many of you have ever had the joy of sitting in the stands at an eighty-five degree humidity-laden swimming pool for an entire Saturday to watch your son swim one event, but it is not the pinnacle of human experience! Not that I blame him, but it did not fit into his schedule very often.

Not having my parents there to cheer my accomplishments had a profound effect on my outlook on life. Somehow, in my mind, I began to think "I must not be good enough." This was not a conscious thought, or even a rational one, but the feeling was there nonetheless. The logical thought that follows: "I must not be good enough" is "I should get better." And the final end to the sequence is: "If I am good enough at this, my parents will come to my game/performance/event."

I never thought this "out loud" in my head, but somehow the idea permeated my entire being. So I practiced. I became proficient at a number of different activities. I played soccer. I became the second highest scorer on the team in intramural basketball. I ran the mile and two mile in track. I ran cross country. I had a whole wall full of ribbons won at different swimming meets. I got good grades. (Well, not stellar, I said I wanted my parents' attention, I didn't say I wanted to work THAT hard for it.) I was in choir, barbershop octet, and played the lead in several plays. The funny thing was that no matter how hard I tried, things never changed—see, there was nothing I could do to alter the situation. It was hardwired into the way my parents were. It was ingrained in the way they looked at life, in the demands on their time, and in the list of priorities that they had. There was nothing I could do. Of course, I didn't realize that until I was much older.

I had lived my life like that for many years—not allowing myself to have weaknesses, viewing faults as something that needed to be eradicated. Practice, practice, practice. I had fed myself the lie that my worth was based on how well I could perform. I didn't realize it, but I kept looking for approval based on what I could do. Kind of a stinky way to find acceptance, huh?

By the time I entered college, this mode of thinking was branded on my brain. It was how I looked at everything. I got involved playing keyboard with the worship band for the Campus Ministry I was involved in. I stunk. Thankfully, the leader had a ton of grace and encouraged me instead of telling me how I really sounded.

Deep down, I knew that I wasn't nearly as good as I could be at keyboard. So I practiced. A lot. I got better. I started to lead worship. I kept working at it and I kept improving. I even took some lessons. I became relatively accomplished and I felt pretty good about myself.

My success with the keyboard emboldened me, and I became more involved with the world of music. I learned to play keyboard and acoustic guitar. Then I learned drums. Then I started to work on bass and electric guitar. I guess I thought I could be a whole band by myself. Unfortunately, I only have two hands and two feet.

After I graduated from college, I went on to lead worship at a local church. I even was signed to a record label. The problem was that I still based how I felt about myself on my performance. If worship went badly on a Sunday, or the people didn't get into worship for whatever reason, I would beat myself up about it at least until Wednesday. "I must not have tried hard enough. I should have done this different." You know the drill. Don't get me wrong, despite these small failures, I didn't think badly about myself, but mainly because I hadn't failed on a grand scale yet. These small failures were only a scathing reminder that I needed to try harder and get better.

Have you ever come to a time in your life where your talent was not enough? I have heard it said: "You can get by on talent for a lot of years, but sooner or later, in order to follow what God wants, you will have to fall into that scary abyss where talent alone cannot carry you." I came to that place.

It was several years later. The design firm that I had founded was barely scraping by, I had begun a new job and moved across the state. Then for some unknown reason, I hit an intensely difficult period in my life. (Actually, that's putting it mildly. If I said what it was truly like, they couldn't put this book in the Inspirational section!) I kept coming face to face with my failings—my shortcomings—my faults.

It seemed that no matter where I turned, there was something I wasn't good at. Everything I tried turned to cowpies. I felt like if I was put in charge of something even a moron couldn't mess up, you know, like boiling water, the water would turn into acid, melt the pan, sear through the stove and undermine the foundation of the house turning it into a smoking ruin! For three generations after, everyone who passed by would point the place out to their children and use it as an example of what happens when kids don't obey their parents. Suffice to say, I was making mistakes. Constantly.

Even in music, something that I was very proficient at, I felt like I was failing. I had a hard time remembering how to play different parts. It felt like my fingers were made of wood. I couldn't remember the words. It seemed that everything that I used to be talented at, I no longer could do. Don't get me wrong, I did OK. The problem was that I wasn't as good as I wanted to be at it. I wasn't perfect.

You see, I was learning a new instrument. Our worship team needed someone to play electric guitar. I had played acoustic guitar for several years and was a pretty good rhythm guitar player. I just didn't know how to play lead electric. I was used to playing chords. Well, the electric has a different tonal structure, so that I even had to learn new chords so that they sounded good. I wasn't used to the guitar, I wasn't used to the amplifier (it made funny sounds when I didn't want it to). I just was having a hard time getting used to this instrument!

On top of that, the business I was running was in the red for over twelve months. We were working our tails off, but it seemed like we were getting nowhere. The clients weren't there, the projects fell apart, and every single month, my wife and I were having to loan the business money, which of course did wonders for our personal finances!

Then, as the final nail in the coffin of my self esteem, someone I respected told me that I didn't have charisma, and that I had a problem keeping rhythm while I led worship! Nothing like a great big pile of stuff that you're not good at to make you feel good about yourself, huh?

I know, I know, I'm an oversensitive artist and I should just get over myself! Believe me, I tried! I practiced until my fingers bled (almost), I prayed, I even offered to give a newborn baby goat as a sacrifice if only I could play well. Actually I didn't (the part about the goat), I just wanted to see if you were paying attention. I didn't realize how much each of these things impacted how I felt about myself and my abilities until one particular event.

Our worship leader was going to be out of town one Sunday, and I was supposed to fill in. It had been months since I had led worship, so I was understandably nervous. I wanted to prove myself. I wanted people to walk away and say, "Wow, that guy can really lead worship!" I wanted everything to go well. Scratch that, I wanted everything to go perfectly!

I wasn't all that sure about myself, so I tried to overcome my fear in the normal way. I practiced for hours each day. I practiced until the blisters on my fingers turned to calluses. I memorized the songs. I could play them with my eyes closed. Finally, on the Friday before I was supposed to lead, I was practicing yet again when a thought came into my head: *Why are you doing this?*

Well, I find it best to answer myself when I talk to me in that tone of voice, so I said: "So that I can do well when I lead worship on Sunday!" The voice in my head said: "You already have all the songs memorized, you already know them like the back of your hand, why are you still practicing?" I resented the tone that I took with myself, so, angrily, I replied: "So I can prove that guy wrong that said I didn't have charisma and that I had a problem with timing!" Then I realized what I had just said.

I was trying to be perfect just so that I could prove one person's opinion of me wrong! I had no joy in leading worship—it was all about me, about proving how talented I was. It wasn't any longer about God and bringing Him praise. It was about me. I couldn't stand that someone saw weakness in me! I couldn't stand seeing weakness in myself.

I knew this was the wrong attitude. So I stopped practicing. I put down my guitar and went out and saw a movie. I gave the situation over to God. I enjoyed my weekend.

Now the fairy tale ending to this story would be that everything went perfectly on Sunday, many people came up to me afterward and congratulated me on doing a good job, and the person that had questioned my abilities approached on bended knee and admitted that he was wrong about me and asked me to forgive him. Notice, however, that this story does not start with the words "Once upon a time."

Practice went well and we were ready. I vocally led a couple of songs, I had another male leader lead a couple of songs that I played electric guitar for and then I switched guitars and a female vocalist did the beginning verse of a slower song. That's how we practiced it. It went as smooth as butter. Unfortunately, that's not how it went during service!

Everything was fine until the slower song. The vocalist started singing in the wrong key. And didn't stop there. She kept singing!

I stood up there trying to figure out what to do, and came to the realization that there really was nothing we could do, we had to keep going. After one time through the verse with the vocalist singing in a different key than the band, we were able to get back on track, but I felt like I had failed. I had not anticipated the problem that we would have with that song and the service did not go as I had planned. I came face to face with my weakness, my failure once again!

Fear and Weakness

In praying about this situation and all of the things that I had come up against that had glaringly shown me that I was not perfect, God put this on my heart. "You are trying so hard to be perfect, but that's what I sent Jesus for. You are not perfect. In not allowing yourself to have weaknesses, you are not allowing me to be strong. If you don't learn to lean on me and embrace those shortcomings, you will never accomplish the things that I have for you—because they are so much bigger that what you alone can do."

I was afraid. I was afraid of my weakness. I was afraid of failing. I was afraid that others would realize that I wasn't perfect. I was afraid that someone would put me up against some imaginary measuring stick and I wouldn't measure up. I guess I was afraid that other people would see me as I see myself.

But God was saying, "Don't worry about measuring up! You don't. If you can embrace yourself as I embrace you, with all of your shortcomings, your failures, your insufficiencies, then you are at the place where I can use you, because you are not relying on your own strength, you are relying on me."

Grace is a hard thing for me, because I feel like I have to earn my own way. I feel like I have to show my value by what I can do. If someone were to try to give me a million dollars, I'm so neurotic I would feel compelled to buy them lunch in order to "repay them" for the gift they've given me! That's probably why I have such a hard time accepting my failures, because it clearly shows me that in no way, shape, or form am I earning my own way!

The problem with having a world-view like mine is this: When we try to earn our own salvation, it cheapens the gift that God gives us. Take the example I just gave about someone giving me a million dollars. How would that person have felt when I said: "Well, let me buy you lunch to repay you for the million dollars that you just gave me?" Cheap. They would have thought: "Is that all my gift is worth to him, a measly lunch? Does he think that makes us even?" How much better would it be to look at that person in the eye and say, "My vocabulary does not have the words to express the thankfulness that I have for this great gift that you've given me, but I will do my best to use it wisely. Thank you!"

There is no way I can make myself worth more to God. God gives me worth. There's no way that I can earn my own salvation. It only comes through Him. He brings strength. The only thing that I bring to the table is weakness, failure and shortcomings. The simple fact of the matter is that God is faithful in and because of our weakness! It is our weakness that beckons and woos His faithfulness.

2 Corinthians 12: 9-10 says:

"Therefore I will boast all the more gladly about my weaknesses, so that Christ's power may rest on me. That is why, for Christ's sake, I delight in weaknesses, in insults, in hardships, in persecutions, in difficulties. For when I am weak, then I am strong." (NIV)

Notice that this verse seems to say that until we allow ourselves to be weak, Christ's power cannot rest on us. Fear of failure should not be a factor. We have already failed! We have already fallen short, so that's done with! It's out of the way and we can move forward to the things God has called us for!

Unless we can accept our ongoing failures, our daily shortcomings and rest in His grace, we can never accomplish the gargantuan tasks that God has for us to succeed in. We will limit ourselves.

Every single person in the Bible that did great things for God had flaws. Look at Peter, Gideon, David, Rahab, and Paul just to name a few. They accomplished these monumental things for two simple reasons:

they were called by God, and they acknowledged their flaws and relied on God's strength.

I am learning to rely on God in the way that those in the Bible did. It's not easy. I am realizing that my strength is in my weakness—in my reliance on Him. I am learning to accept myself: the good, the bad, the strengths, and yes, the flaws. I am trying hard not to push myself for perfection. I am walking the hard road of Grace and God has shown Himself faithful with every step.

The Faithfulness of a Nap

I had a friend named Danforth. I met him in college and he was the polar opposite of me. I am an incredibly driven, goals oriented, type A personality. He was the most gentle, calm, take-life-as-it-comes person on the face of the earth. He drove me crazy!

Danforth would come into the room (usually about 15 minutes late) in his Birkenstocks and wool socks. His hair was kind of a blondish brown and curly. Somehow it looked neat and messy at the same time. He had little round glasses and wore 14 layers of clothing—even in summer. He would be carrying his guitar and his backpack. His bag had doodles on it and was filled with about 30 more things than you could fit in the trunk of a Buick! But he would sit down and smile and you would forget all about his appearance and for some reason start to think about heaven.

I think Dan was closer to heaven than most. There was just something different about the way he looked at everything. He had a brightness about him. He would get so excited when he talked about Jesus and when he would tell you about his prayers, you got the feeling that probably Jesus just dropped by, and they had a good conversation! Dan inexplicably moved outside of the realm of the space/time continuum.

Danforth was deliberate about everything. He thought long and hard about whether to have peas or carrots as the vegetable with his dinner. He drove 10 miles an hour under the speed limit (I assume in order to watch for turtles, just in case one of them was out for an afternoon stroll). If you asked him if he wanted to go somewhere with you, he would ponder it, weighing the pros and cons and six hours later he would give you an answer. By this time, the event was over, but what could you do? It was just how Danforth was.

You see, Danforth died recently. It was like he was so close to heaven that he finally took that last little step and there he was at heaven's door telling St. Pete about his good friend Jesus.

Death strikes you in a funny way. You never know how you will react. When a friend of mine called me to let me know about Dan's death, my response was, "Well, that's not good!" I then thought that maybe a flip comment wasn't the most supportive at the time. So, I asked how it happened. Maybe funny comments are my defense mechanism. Maybe I was in shock. Or maybe that's how I really felt. That Danforth's death wasn't good—for me, for his family, or for the friend that had called. It was good for Danforth though.

Dan was a hemophiliac and had gotten a batch of bad blood before they started testing for the HIV virus. When I met him, the dichotomy struck me with force—here was this person with death in his body, but at the same time, he was one of the most alive people that I knew. He had plans for the future. He got his college degree, but I'm not sure what it was in. You know, I don't even know if he cared what his degree was. That wasn't the point. The point for Danforth was ministry—serving others. He wanted to be "about something."

All through college, he served. He was on the worship team for the campus ministry we were in. He was a small group leader. He was always helping someone else, giving them a ride, showing them how to do something, or just listening. He was the most intense listener! He would stare right at you while you spoke to him and you got the feeling that there was nothing more important in the world to him than to hear what you were going to say next. He helped others. He just wanted to make other people feel important. And he didn't stop after he graduated from college.

He went into campus ministry and was a campus pastor for many years. That was his goal in life. Most people want to achieve things—get nice cars, or houses, or have a great job. His goal was to serve God. Period. We would drive around in his three-cylinder car (yes, only three cylinders), and work on fund raisers for the ministry. Or go to worship team practice. Or Bible study, or prayer. In the interest of full disclosure, though, I can say that even though serving God was Danforth's only goal, it wasn't his only desire.

I remember one time as we talked, he told me how he really wanted to get married and have kids. I agreed with his faith verbally, but inside I thought: "What, are you nuts? How can you have kids when you have HIV?" But you know what, God granted him a wonderful wife and five children. Five! Talk about God doing over and above what we could ask or imagine! And Danforth's life was complete.

He was the one that taught me about completeness and satisfaction. Our views of the world were so different, his actions would constantly make me reassess my view of the world. Which is a nice way of saying that his actions made me want to pull out my hair, stuff it into my mouth and scream! I would want to go faster, he would want to go slower. I would push ahead and he would pull back. I found myself looking at each decision differently because of his method of doing things. At the time I didn't realize how much this made me grow, I just knew how much this frustrated me!

I remember one time, we were serving together on the worship team. He was the leader and played guitar, and I was one of the worship team members and played keyboard. We were working on redoing the worship music folder and getting it organized. We were entering all the songs into the computer and making a database. Then we printed out the songs and put them into the folders. It was a task that took several weeks. We had worked about an hour and I had to go to class. He was going to work until I got back. Then we would begin to assemble the folders.

I went to class. I was in graphic design school at the time, so there wasn't a lot of hard science, but it was a grueling degree nonetheless. We would spend countless hours working on projects and our classes consisted of critiques, meetings, and presentations. So, there I was, in class for two long hours, suffering the indignities of having someone else tell me why my design work was sub-par; something about that didn't put me in the best frame of mind!

I came back to my apartment after that wonderful experience, fully expecting to find considerable progress made on the reorganization of the worship folder. What I found instead was Danforth, napping on my floor.

I was a little put out. Here I was, working my tail off, going to class and what was he doing? Napping! So I said, "What are you doing?" These were the words that I chose to replace what I was thinking! He said, "I was taking a nap." I'm thinking: "Yes, I can see that, but how is your wonderful nap helping to get the stinking work done!?"

He went on to tell me that as he was working, he got kind of tired so he decided to lay down for a while. I could not understand him! In my world, you don't go to sleep when you have made a commitment to finish something! You didn't quit until it was done. His way of reasoning was so much different than mine! I decided to be a good "Christian" and forgive him, though. Wasn't that incredibly kind and hypocritical of me? Yea, me!

I know, some of you are thinking: "Forgive him for what? He didn't do anything wrong." That's the entire point. He didn't do anything wrong. The problem was with me, not with him. As I thought about it, I realized that I needed to be more like Danforth, not try to make him more like me. If we would have been Biblical characters, he would have been Mary (except without the dress), being commended for sitting at Jesus' feet and I would have been the frustrated Martha trying to do the dishes, cook the meal, and check her email.

Our relationship was dotted with many different such instances. Some of them bringing incredible angst, but each of them driving home the lesson of how I needed to be. I needed to recognize and appreciate the times when it was the moment to take a nap instead of pushing full-boar. I needed to seek God instead of just being task oriented. I needed to go slower and appreciate the journey, not just the goal. As time went on, the frustration with Danforth became less and less, and my love and respect for him deepened. I was learning the lessons God wanted me to learn.

Finally, I had ingested enough of the character that God wanted me to have that when Danforth didn't show up at my house on time, I wasn't frustrated. When he was two hours late, I wasn't stressed. When he called and said, "I'm not at your house yet." I just laughed and asked what happened. He said, "I was tired, so I pulled over and took a nap."

God was so faithful in Danforth's life. As I watched how God turned up again and again and I saw the unshakeable faith that he had, I realized that I wanted that. Danforth loved God with all his heart! When I talked to him about a month before he died, he prayed for me. His speech was slurred, he couldn't really say what he meant, but he prayed for me. Even then, he couldn't stop talking about how faithful God was in his life.

I had a hard time making my voice press past the lump in my throat because I knew that Danforth was getting ready to take a nap for the final time and yet he cared more about me than he cared about his own problems! He wanted to make sure that I was all right. He checked on my marriage, my kids. He affirmed me and brought light into our conversation. As I reciprocated and prayed for him, I felt like my prayer was a vacuous empty space when I compared it to the fullness of Dan's love for God!

We said goodbye and I thought that Danforth was not long in this world. I heard later that he rallied and actually went home! Then, about two months later, I got the call that he had passed away. He really had gone home. Danforth was one of those rare individuals that was never really comfortable in this fast-paced world that we live in. He was like a foot crammed into a shoe two sizes too small. I understand why now. He was made for heaven.

Danforth and a friend wrote a song about faith. We used to sing it in campus ministry. It was a bluesy tune that talked about the heroes of faith. And like everything that Danforth did, it was a little different. It had about ten verses, and it seemed like he was making up new ones all the time—but somehow, the song just fit him perfectly.

Abel, Enoch, Noah, Abraham,

Isaac, Jacob, and Moses too

Sarah and Samuel, Rahab and Me and You

They lived by faith, and not by sight.

The song went on to describe faith and I think the only thing missing was Danforth's name.

You see, right up to the time of his death, Danforth believed for his healing. And he got it. Today he is dancing and singing with the One he loves so well—disease free, and able to spend as much time doing all the things that he wants to do! And as I think about the picture of Danforth walking with Jesus, talking about why the sky is a certain color, I can't help but think: "There is a faithful God!"

Resting in God

I try too hard! I work constantly. When I am sitting on the couch, watching a movie, I am probably also checking my email, playing a game and talking on the phone. I think I might be a "stimulation addict." (I know, there probably isn't such a thing, but if there was, I would be one!) I have done it enough to know that it doesn't accomplish more, it just increases my frustration.

The biggest thing knowing Danforth has taught me about God's faithfulness is that there is a time to rest. To wait. To trust. Take a look at how God created the universe. On the seventh day, He rested. Jesus, himself, often went off into the wilderness to spend time alone. These times of rest are just as important and sometimes more important than the times of hard charging, moving forward, and pressing on with all your might.

In Christianity there is balance. God's faithfulness will always be there. I realized that because of Danforth's example, my busyness didn't come from a desire to please God, it came out of a need to prove my worth. The interesting thing is that my worth doesn't come from what I can do anyway. It comes from the faithfulness of God. The more that I spend time with Him, the more I feel valued. The less I know Him, the more I find myself pushing too hard toward some ill-defined goal and ending up frustrated to the point of hara-kiri. I miss out on so much when I just push ahead as hard as I can and I don't take time to wait on God.

The third chapter of Ecclesiastes verses 1-8 puts it well.

"There is a time for everything,
and a season for every activity under heaven:
a time to be born and a time to die,
a time to plant and a time to uproot,
a time to kill and a time to heal,
a time to tear down and a time to build,
a time to weep and a time to laugh,
a time to mourn and a time to dance,
a time to scatter stones and a time to gather them,
a time to embrace and a time to refrain,
a time to search and a time to give up,
a time to keep and a time to throw away,
a time to tear and a time to mend,
a time to be silent and a time to speak,
a time to love and a time to hate,
a time for war and a time for peace." (NIV)

This verse has been used to the point of numbness, but stop for a moment and think about the truth in it. There is a time to rest, a time to be silent, a time to be still and know that He is God.

This balance for our spirits is so important! If we are always charging ahead, there is no time for Him to speak into our lives—because He speaks in a soft voice. But on the other side of the equation, if we only sit and "rest in Him," we will never accomplish His goals for our lives.

Look at the story of Mary and Martha in Luke 10. So many times we hear about Mary and how she chose "the better path." When I was younger, I thought, "Man, she was being lazy! Why in the world would Jesus commend her for that?" As I have pondered this through the years however, I have come to a different conclusion. I truly don't believe that Mary was a lazy person. This was the same person who poured out the perfume on Jesus' feet and wiped them with her hair.

I believe that Mary was as hard a worker as her sister Martha, but the difference was that she knew the appropriate time to "rest." Luke 10:40 says, "But Martha was distracted by all of the preparations that had to be made." (NIV) Later, in verses 41 and 42, it says, "Martha, Martha," the Lord answered, "you are worried and upset about many things, but only one thing is needed. Mary has chosen what is better, and it will not be taken away from her." (NIV) In these verses, there are two words that stuck out to me. The first is the word "distracted" and the second is the word "chosen."

Martha was distracted. She allowed the things that she "had" to do come in the way of the thing that was needful at that time. Mary chose to rest in the Lord. She saw all the same things that cried out to be done, but she understood that now was not the time for her to do them. Now was the time to rest and listen to Jesus.

I so badly want to choose, like Mary to rest in the Lord, but it is hard. I know God is faithful, but when I am moving so fast in my everyday life, I have a hard time focusing on the ways that He shows His faithfulness. Honestly, I have to admit many times I allow myself to be distracted like Martha instead.

It is hard to take the time to rest in today's fast-paced society. Everywhere you go, the world is telling us to go faster. We have fast cars, fast food, fast credit approval! The reason that Danforth stuck out so much from the rest of us was because he understood the importance of a nap!

Often, I will be distracted by all of the reasons that I can't "take a nap," can't rest in God, can't wait on the Lord, rather than choosing to take the time to allow God's faithfulness to speak to me. I am slowly learning though, that the resting is just as important as the "important stuff." Danforth taught me that. Thanks, Danforth.

Locusts Eat More Than Teenagers

I was in my late twenties and we had purchased our first luxury car. I have to admit it was a bit of a heady experience. I'm not sure I was ever arrogant enough as a kid to think "Someday I'm going to drive a really nice car," but I have to tell you that as I sat in the leather-seated luxury, I felt very much at home! And as the salesman took us out for a drive and lulled us into a state of unrelenting need, my ego was singing. And when we went to pick up the car and my four-year-old son got in and exclaimed, "Wow, we've never had a car like this one before!" To which the salesman answered: "Most people have never had a car like this before," (he must have been well trained), my ego hit the high note!

Now before you send me letters chastising me for my unwise use of God's money, let me just say this—we bought the car out of necessity. Really. In my industry (advertising), there is a certain expectation as to the type of vehicle that you should have. You just have to drive up in a car that announces you and a beat-up old Ford just doesn't cut it. At least that is what I told other people. We also found that because we lived on a dirt road, we needed a car with all-wheel drive, right? (Sense the rationalization?)

But, in the interest of being completely honest, I would have to say that I took the winding path into luxury vehicles for no other reason than because I wanted to. Some guilty part of me craved what that vehicle said about me. It said "We've arrived." It was a step above. It drove smoothly, had a beautiful interior and more buttons than I knew what to do with. And, have mercy, when you stepped on the gas, it pushed you into your seat like a sumo wrestler who thinks you're cutting in front of him at the buffet line! (If you are a law enforcement officer, please skip to the next paragraph, thank you.) I found myself driving quite a bit faster than the posted speed limit. "What, you mean it's not just a recommendation?"

Just so that you don't think me to be completely frivolous, I should tell you that we bought our luxury car used. We couldn't afford to buy one new. Nevertheless, our new (used) car had a 40,000 mile warranty—which was good, because it was very expensive to fix! I mean VERY expensive! I think they must have fashioned the bolts for this vehicle out of pure gold and then set a diamond stud in each one! So you can imagine, it was a rather disconcerting sensation when things started to break.

And things kept going wrong. First, the turbo broke down. Then, it needed new brakes and rotors, then it was this or that. All in all, there was about $6,000 in repairs that needed to be made to the vehicle in the first year. It seemed like I was at the dealership at least once a month. I think they were ready to give me my own desk and phone! Fortunately, these were all covered under the warranty—which was lucky for us. You would think that I would have taken all those things breaking as a sign to find a different car, wouldn't you? But no, I was blindly oblivious to anything wrong with my "precious car." All of that changed abruptly, though, in the sultry month of August.

I was on a business trip in Indiana. I was going on a week-long photo shoot at a camp in the middle of nowhere. I had brought along another person from our design firm and we embarked on the long journey to Podunkville (if there is actually a place named that, and you happen to live there, I sincerely apologize). It was an eight-hour journey through some of the flattest land conceivable on a round planet.

We were approximately seven miles from the camp, on a road that was just one step up from a two-track when the engine started losing power. I accelerated, but nothing happened. I tried turning off all of the electronic devices in the car—nothing. I prayed. Still nothing! I prayed louder just in case God was listening to His tunes and couldn't hear me. No answer! Slowly, unceasingly, we were gliding to an ignominious stop between a ditch, a cornfield and a dilapidated barn.

I could hear the crickets chirping and knew that I couldn't sit there and ponder the wondrous lack of scenery forever. I mean, my co-worker was staring at me with a horrified look on her face! Now, I am about as mechanically minded as a Cro-Magnon man looking at a jet engine, but I knew the protocol. It's in "The Big Book of Rules for Social Behavior of Homo Sapien Males." On page 42, it says "When a male finds himself in a situation whereby his mode of transportation (i.e. car) has broken down, said male should immediately proceed to the front of the vehicle, open the hood, and gaze at the engine while making appropriate thought-process noises. (See also "Male Posturing.")"

I know nothing about cars. I can tell you where to put the gas in, and if I were held at gunpoint, I could probably change the oil, but my expertise takes an abrupt nosedive off the cliff of ignorance at that point! But rules are rules. So, I popped the hood and went to look at the engine. Did you know in an engine there are a lot of parts that can break off in your hands for no apparent reason? Just kidding, I didn't touch anything because I didn't want to disturb the "crime scene" for the mechanic. Actually, it was because I didn't know what in the world I was doing!

After an appropriate amount of time pretending to fiddle with the engine, including several times of trying to start the engine and failing, I called a spade a spade, pronounced it a dead issue and called a tow truck.

So there we were, in the middle of a cornfield, seven miles from the nearest city, 500 miles from home, the sun throwing ninety-six degree rays at us, with no transportation! Sounds fun like a trip to the dentist, huh? My co-worker turned to look at me and said "I'm going to get a car JUST like this!" I had to hold myself back from firing her on the spot!

I don't know what it is about people from that area, but they all are very nice. The tow-truck man that picked us up had a son that was a professional wrestler (no joke), and spent the whole twenty-five minute trip to the garage regaling us with tales about his son's wrestling career! I do have to say though, he had a full compliment of teeth, smelled reasonably neutral, and was as gentle and kind as could be. Guess the stereotypes are wrong. Anyway, he took us to the hotel and the car went to a garage that he recommended.

We still had a photo shoot that needed to be done, so we made arrangements to borrow a car and go to the camp so that we could get to work. The camp is situated on about 750 acres of wooded hilly terrain, centered around a large lake. They have about 5,000 campers from age seven to fifteen per summer! It was beautiful! The week went wonderfully, we had a great time taking pictures while sliding down ziplines, climbing towers, and kayaking. The weather was perfect and the food was even edible! Then I got the bad news.

The timing belt on my car had broken. Now, I don't know exactly what that means, but it sounded really bad. Actually, the term "timing belt" sounded pretty innocuous, but the mechanic's tone of voice told me that I was in big trouble!

Well, because of its' wonderful German engineering, when the timing belt had blown apart like an overfilled balloon, it had torn apart all of the "small parts of the engine." (Do you like the way that I use technical jargon without fear?) The lifters (whatever those are) had to be replaced and basically, the entire engine had to be rebuilt! Well, that wasn't good news!

To recap: my luxury car had broken down, the engine needed to be rebuilt, it would cost about $2800, I was stuck 500 miles from home, we were two hours from the nearest airport, I had a business associate with me, and it would take at least two weeks to fix. And since I was at the tail-end of my business trip, the only options were to live in a Quonset hut at the camp and eat bugs and worms, or to figure out some alternate way to get home! Aaaaarrrrggg!

After the initial shock wore off, I made some plans. Here was the grand scheme: I would rent a car, drive it back to Michigan, come back in two weeks when the car was fixed, return the rental, and drive home in my newly renovated vehicle.

Sounds simple, right? Well it wasn't nearly as straightforward as I would have liked. I failed to take into account the rental costs if the repairs took over two weeks to complete, which they did. The place I rented the car from was local, so I HAD to return the car to the same location, and I got really busy, so I really didn't have time to make the trip. In the meantime, I found out someone was coming north from the camp and could have brought up my car, except then I was stuck with the rental! Quite a conundrum!

I finally got everything figured out and the rental went back to Indiana and I was again stuck with my "beloved" luxury car, but I was still out the money for the rental and the repairs. All told, I spent about $3400, not to mention mental anguish, embarrassment and all of the other fun stuff that goes along with it! I was not, however, thinking about suing, so everything but the money was considered inconsequential. Now I know that you all have large amounts of cash laying around for just such instances, but I didn't, so needless to say I was not very happy. Fortunately, God was watching out for me.

We kept that car about a year after the "big breakdown," and it continued to give us problems. Finally, we traded it in for a bigger vehicle with less mileage, and didn't think any more about it. Until about two years after that incident, we got a letter from the car manufacturer stating that they were addressing customer complaints about the timing belt on the car we owned and would cover the cost of replacing the timing belt if it was needed! They would also reimburse any repairs that were necessary because of timing belt failure! Hmmm…

After running around the house like a madman yelling at the top of my lungs, I rummaged through my receipts (for once being anal retentive paid off), and filled out all the forms. I then sent in the request for reimbursement, scarcely daring to believe that it could really be that easy. Guess what? About six weeks later, we got a check for about $3400! This was the reimbursement for a repair that happened over two years ago, and a reminder that God is able to restore even those things that we think are gone forever!

God Restores

God is able to restore. It doesn't matter if it is lost innocence, lost money, or lost relationships. God can restore. In Joel 2:25, it says: "I will repay you for the years the locusts have eaten." (NIV) while this is a specific prophecy, there is an eternal principle that can be taken from it. God works for the benefit of His people. His faithfulness extends beyond the realm of time and works behind the veil of the seen. He is not bound by what human minds think is possible, so when He says He will restore, it doesn't matter how big the loss is, or how hurtful the tragedy, He can make it better!

If you look the natural world, and apply the power of God to it, you will see what I mean. I heard a statistic a while ago about people who are extremely rich. They found that this type of person, on average, goes bankrupt three times. Three times! Now I know you are saying: "Oh great, now he's telling us how easy it is for us to lose our money!" No, what I am saying is this: when a very rich person goes bankrupt the first time, what do you think goes through their mind? Not ever having been in this situation, I can only conjecture, but I would consider it the end of the world. I would think; "I worked so hard to amass this wealth and it's gone! I might as well go live with the pygmies in Africa, I wonder where one can purchase a good loincloth!" I would believe that there was no way out of that situation.

What if somehow I make my fortune back and I make more money on top of that? Then I lose it—again! What am I thinking now? "Well, that was fun, boy, money sure is fleeting! Guess I'll have to try again." One more time I gain and lose a fortune. What are my thoughts now? I come to a place where I realize that no matter how much I gain and lose, it can be restored. No matter how bleak the situation looks, it can get better. This is the type of trust and belief that we need to have in God. We need to be able to counteract that doubt in our believing hearts with the deep knowledge that no matter what was stolen, ripped away, beaten out of us or given up, that God is able to restore!

When we throw ourselves, fully trusting, into the net of God's faithfulness, He will not fail us. Elsewhere in the Bible it says; "And we know that in all things God works for the good of those who love Him, who have been called according to His purpose." (Rom. 8:28 NIV) God is able to restore the things that you have lost. The key is trust.

Things will not turn out the way you think they should. In the story about my ill-fated luxury car, wouldn't it have been better to keep my car from ever breaking down? Wouldn't it have been easier for God to show His faithfulness by miraculously "healing" my car when I prayed? Wouldn't it have made more sense to somehow make the repair free, and make it able to be done on the spot? Yes, to my limited mind, that seems a lot better. Yet, God chose to do it the way He did.

Often, I look at things through my puny little window of understanding and I am completely bummed out because God allowed my car to break down, or a friend is mad at me, or there are troubles in my marriage. I'm not saying that my problems are not real, but the bottom line is that God is bigger than any problem, situation, or hurt that is in my life—and if I will allow Him, and if I will trust Him, he is able to restore even those things that I thought were lost forever!

It says in the Bible that in this life we will have troubles. (John 16:33) It's part of being human. We live in a fallen world. Things go wrong, we sin, people hurt us. The important thing to remember is this: "Because of God's faithfulness, the end of the story isn't written yet."

Here's what that means: Satan is going to try to steal, kill and destroy. (John 10:10) He may destroy a relationship like a marriage or a friendship. He may entice you into a risky business venture and steal your money. He may kill your innocence. And years after all of these things are said and done, Satan will whisper in your ear. He will say; "It's your fault all of these things happened. God isn't with you. He doesn't care about you, or He would never have let them happen in the first place." If you don't counteract these lies with the truth, you will start to accept them as fact. Don't believe them!

You can choose to believe that God is faithful. You can choose to trust in the fact that God is able to restore. And because of these two bedrock truths, you can choose to move on. Yes, we make mistakes. Should I have bought the luxury car in the first place? Maybe, maybe not, but if it was a mistake, the one thing that God did prove through this is that His ability to restore is bigger than our mistakes. In fact His ability to rebuild is so much bigger than our screwups, it's like comparing an ant to an elephant.

Don't let Satan's lies keep you from being effective for God! It says that a thousand years are like a moment to God and what that means is this; God's memory is long. Even when we have forgotten, He has not. He remembers the tears and frustration as you cried on His shoulder and just like any father, He looks for a way to make it better. As we give the situation to Him, that allows Him freedom to deal with it in the way that He sees fit. God can restore your innocence. God can restore your financial position. God can restore your marriage. Because while everything changes around us, there is one bedrock truth; God is faithful.

Your Daddy Loves You

Do you remember those days in high school? Sitting in that hot, humid room listening to the teacher drone on about the value of cosine or participial phrases? Wondering if the love of your life would gift you with a fleeting glance in the hallway? Remember the pimples, the social humiliation, the agony not fitting in and not standing out? Ah, the good old days.

If only raising children was as easy as high school with all of its' pitfalls. If only there was a 678 page book that you could study, or a "multiple guess" test you could take. But no. That would be too easy. Raising kids seems to be all experiential learning, folks.

You see, these small bundles of "joy" don't come with any instruction manual, return policy, or warning label. If you aren't careful, you will find yourself up to your eyeballs in dirty diapers and spit up so fast it will make your head spin.

To me, the first years of a baby's existence are the most boring. (I know, I'm not supposed to say that, because those are the years that are "magical." Please forgive me.) That's the way I feel though. I am an active person. I like doing things, and let's be honest, how exciting is it sitting around the living room seeing how long it will be before that string of drool hits the floor?

I had friends that would sit there for hours and take bets on how long it would take their child to fall over when he was in a sitting position. Don't tell me that's exciting! By the way, don't worry, their child is in therapy now and progressing nicely.

Now that my children are grown a bit more though, and running through the house playing Jedi Warriors, I long for the days when the only sound they made was a gentle cooing as they spit up on my shoulder!

Caleb was our first child. Poor boy. As a result, our expectations of him were a bit high. I was very disappointed when he was not speaking by the age of two—in French. I mean, I don't know French, so I figured that the least he could do is learn it and teach me—after all, I am paying for his food and clothes! It seemed like a fair trade.

Unfortunately, mostly what he did at first was eat and poop. I kind of felt like a kid that got something for Christmas that he had been hoping for the whole year. After about an hour of playing with him, I was kind of thinking; "Is that all it does?" Fortunately, he grew pretty quickly, and really began to take on a personality all his own.

And as Caleb grew, he began to teach me things—strange things. Did you know that every single rock is unique and special? I can prove it to you, because he brought me every stone in the northern hemisphere and expected me to treasure them like jewels! I did. He taught me that it is not good to feed a baby spicy food—at least without a gross of diapers lying around. Did you know that you should never take Ny-Quill and try to change a baby at 3 am? Another important lesson from Caleb.

Actually, having our first child taught me a lot of really good things too. I became more patient, caring, and less narcissistic. (I'm still working on that last one.) I learned the value of pouring love into someone else and having that love reflected back to me. I began to understand what a difference a good dad can make in a child's life, and what a disastrous impact an indifferent father can have on a child. Mostly, though, Caleb made me want to be a better dad, a better husband, a better person.

One of the neatest things that Caleb showed me had to do with how God looks at us. It was one of those perfect days that only come during the month of August. It had been a sultry summer, dotted with many outdoor activities, all thoroughly enjoyable. The sky was clear with only a brushstroke of a cloud for an artistic touch, the temperature was a perfect seventy-six degrees with low humidity, and the only thing that marred the peaceful serenity was the knowledge that we would soon be heading into fall. I chose not to worry about that then, because, after all, I had a perfect day.

Pam and I both worked, with her gone a couple of days a week and me putting in a little less than 40 hours. We had chosen a lighter working schedule for both of us so that we had more time to be with Caleb. We really didn't want him to have to be in daycare full time. On the days she did have to work, one of our dear friends who was like a grandma to Caleb watched him—talk about a perfect situation!

Anyway, I had just picked Caleb up from our friend's house after work. He was two years old and of course we had him in a twelve-point harness in the exact middle of the back seat—to protect him. We further secured his safety with two rolls of duct tape and foam padding. In reality, we just had him in a car seat; it just seemed like a lot more when we were trying to wrestle him in and out of that medieval torture device!

We were driving home, just Caleb and me, he was in the back seat and I was in the drivers seat (of course). At the time, we had a car that had a sunroof in it. The late afternoon sun was pouring its' warmth through the portal and falling gently on his face. I had stopped at a stop sign and just happened to turn around and glance back at him.

The light had framed his face and given him an angelic glow. His hair, at that age, never seemed to lie down and so it stuck straight up like wheat and caught the light and reflected it back. His whole body was bathed in warmth, and in that moment he looked at me—at his daddy and knew me. You could see the recognition spread across his face. He knew I was his dad! And he was proud that I was his dad! As a huge smile spread across his face, I could see the excitement in his eyes that I belonged to him, and I knew that in that moment, the only thing that he wanted was to be with me.

I was frozen. A feeling that I had never had before welled up inside of me. I gulped back tears and just soaked in that smile. I wanted to say so many things to him. Things like, "I want to be there to help you learn to ride a bike. I want to hold you when your girlfriend breaks your heart. I want to watch you as you play sports. I want to pay for your college—I'm not sure how. I want to be there for the good times, the bad times, through your triumphs and failures. I want you to know how special I think you are, and how my heart longs to see you succeed. I want you to share everything with me!"

I wanted to tell him all about life—all the things I had learned and the mistakes I had made. I wanted to give him everything that I knew would help him in life. I wanted to protect him from pain, I wanted to teach him how to do things that my dad never taught me. I wanted to tell him the secrets of the universe. But all those things just stuck in my throat, and what ended up coming out were these four simple words: "Your daddy loves you."

Just four words. "Your daddy loves you." But those words were spoken with the force of all of my feelings, emotions and thoughts behind them. When I said those words, I meant "I want to be there for you." I meant "I want to protect you." I meant "I want to share my life with you and teach you everything that I know." Just four simple words, but they shouted with the force of the intentions and emotions behind them. And right then, I knew what God feels like.

You see, God tell us that He loves us. His word says, "The Lord, your God is with you, He is mighty to save, He will take great delight in you, He will dance over you with singing." (Zeph. 3:17 NIV) If that's not saying "I love you," then I don't know what is! But here's the thing.

When God says, "Your daddy loves you," He means all those other things that I meant when I said it to Caleb as well. He means: "I want to be there for you always. I want to hold you when you are at your lowest. I want to wipe the tears from your eyes. I want you to know that you are so special to me—that in all of creation, there has never been anyone like you. I want to be there as you learn to stand, to trust, to walk, to fall. I care so much about you I would sacrifice anything to be with you—even my own flesh and blood." He means all those things, but it's all encompassed in that simple phrase: "Your daddy loves you."

God's Faithful Love

There were two things God taught me that day about His love. The first was how all encompassing it is when He says that He loves us and the second is about the passion that undergirds His love.

We talk a lot about God's love and the faithfulness of His love. We talk about it so much, in fact, that it becomes an abstract thing. It's like we think, "Out there somewhere, floating in space, maybe in the vicinity of the Orion galaxy, is God's love. It is like a fog that circles my head and brushes up against me sometimes and if I squint my eyes and look hard enough, I can almost see it." We have taken His love and made it into a cold and clinical experience, all antiseptic and coated in white. That's not what His love is like at all!

The lesson that God taught me about His faithful love through that day in August with my son was this: the love of God is passionate. It has emotion just bursting out of it. I imagine, just like when I watch my son at a soccer game score a goal, there are times that God, in His infinite majesty and grandeur jumps up and down in heaven and yells at the top of His lungs for us. He calls out to the angels; "Did you just see what my son just did?! I taught him that! That's my kid! I'm so proud of him!" There are times when God can barely hold back his tears of joy when we look at him with our hands lifted up and say, "Dad, I love you so much." And I know there are times when He has to almost physically hold himself back because He wants to crush that person who just hurt his son.

Because of the passion raging behind God's faithful love, one thing we have to realize is that His love is not a tame little kitten that you can carry around and stroke every once in a while to make you feel better about yourself. God's love is like a jungle cat. It can't be caged, or even predicted at times. There is an air of danger around it because it is so much stronger than you are. It is something you are always aware of. You sense its breath on you when you walk away and you feel its watchful eyes when you begin to stray off the path. You are helpless to its ravages.

And ravage you it will. The heat of His passion for you to succeed will buffet you. He allows you to walk hard paths to strengthen your feet.

Your victories will be hard-won, because he will allow you to fight against towering opponents. But just like a mother lion watches over her cub with fierce pride, so He watches over you with tenderness, grace and fury! And the whole time you are ravaged by the love of an awesome God, you will be so thankful that He always, always works for your benefit.

There's a description of God in the book *The Lion, the Witch and the Wardrobe* by C.S. Lewis that is so appropriate to explain God's love:

"Aslan a man!" said Mr. Beaver sternly. "Certainly not. I tell you he is the King of the wood and the son of the great emperor-beyond-the-Sea. Don't you know who is the King of Beasts? Aslan is a lion—the Lion, the great Lion."

"Ooh!" said Susan, "I'd thought he was a man. Is he—quite safe? I shall feel rather nervous about meeting a lion."

"That you will, dearie, and no mistake," said Mrs. Beaver; "if there's anyone who can appear before Aslan without their knees knocking, they're either braver than most or else just silly."

"Then he isn't safe?" said Lucy."

"Safe?" said Mr. Beaver, "don't you hear what Mrs. Beaver tells you? Who said anything about safe? 'Course he isn't safe. But he's good. He's the King, I tell you."

This description of Aslan could just as well be applied to God's love. "Safe? Who said anything about safe? 'Course it isn't safe. But it's good."

This view of God's passionate love may be unsettling for you, but make no mistake, if you truly grab ahold of this love, it will change you! See, the emotion and passion behind God's love are an awesome thing. They wake us from our lethargy and give us the strength to press on. They take the good and complete plans that God has for us and give them the lasting power to finish.

When God says, "Your daddy loves you," He means that He wants to passionately protect you, ardently hold you, savagely cheer you on, and eagerly provide for your every need. His passion and the completeness of His love go hand in hand.

The second thing that God taught me about His love has to do with its completeness. We use the word love so loosely today. We apply it to bath soap and food and even professional sports games. God does not say, "I love you" loosely. He says it specifically. He says it with force of will.

Just like the words, "Your daddy loves you" to Caleb carried so much other meaning about my hopes, dreams and plans for him; in the same way God's expression of the same phrase carry the same things, except on an infinitely greater scale.

When God says, "I love you" He means, "I want to protect you, I want you to do well, I want to hold you when you cry, and I want to provide every single thing you need." His expression of love, is action. In those three simple words, He commits himself to put all of His resources to work for your benefit.

Now think about what that means. Because He owns everything, knows everything and made everything, nothing is out of the question. If, in His love and knowledge of you, He knew that it would be to your benefit to have every dog in the world follow you around dancing the tango, (though why that would be to your benefit is beyond me), guess what? He would make it happen.

So, what does that mean for your financial situation? Your future plans? Your relationships? It means that because of God's passion and the completeness of His love, nothing, and I mean nothing is impossible! We just have to trust Him and follow where His love leads us.

After that afternoon in the car, I went home and wrote a song about the Father's love for us. It's called "Caleb's Song."

CALEB'S SONG
(Your Daddy Loves You)
A smiling face and trusting eyes
Overwhelmed with love
Innocence in its purity
Pouring from above
And I think of all these things to say to you

They're just overused platitudes
They just don't seem right

So I say, Your daddy loves you
He will never let you fall
He will hold your tiny hand as you grow so tall
Your daddy loves you
He will never let you go
He would sacrifice His life
Your daddy loves you so

Like a child learning to walk
I have fallen again
Looking up with tears on my cheeks
You lift me out of my sin
And you wrap me in your loving embrace
Comforted by the glow of your face
You restore me

'Cause in this changing world of insecurity
Only one thing's sure, my daddy's love for me

And my Daddy loves me
He will never let me fall
He will hold my tiny hand as I grow so tall
My Daddy loves me
He will never let me go
He has sacrificed His life
My Daddy loves me so

Sowing and Reaping Pizzas

I think pizza may be one of nature's perfect foods. I mean think about it, you get vegetables (tomato sauce), dairy (cheese), meat (pepperoni), and a good dose of carbohydrates in the crust! I know it's not the most healthy choice for dinner, but for some reason I find myself craving it from time to time. I wish you could plant a "pizza seed" and in five minutes a pizza would sprout! But since there seem to be twelve pizza places on each block in our town, it's almost as convenient as having your own "pizza tree."

I had gotten no paycheck for about eight months. I was working sixty hours a week, stressed to the max, and was essential to the survival of the design company that I owned, I just didn't get paid. Pam and I had divested ourselves of all earthly wealth in order to keep the business afloat. I was thinking about selling a kidney, but I couldn't figure out a way to do it without surgery, and from what I hear, in most countries, it's relatively illegal, so that really wasn't a viable option.

We had adopted a girl, so now we had two kids to provide for, two house payments and two car payments not to mention niceties like food, water and heat! We were up to our eyeballs in debt, and as a special added boost to my ego, despite all of my hard work, I was contributing nothing, nada, zero to the financial goodie pot! I can't say that I was feeling all that good about myself as a provider for my family, but I guess the point wasn't to make me feel good about myself.

Pam brought in enough to cover one house payment, most of the groceries, and the car payment. She was also picking up extra hours as much as possible, but it still wasn't enough. There was a gap as wide as the Grand Canyon at the end of the month between our income and our expenses!

About that time, our church started to teach on the principle of sowing and reaping. (Great timing, huh? They start talking about giving when you don't even have enough to meet your own bills!) Anyway, this principle is based on the passage in the Bible that reads, "A man reaps what he sows." (Gal. 6:7 NIV) and, "He who sows sparingly will also reap sparingly, and whoever sows generously will also reap generously." (2 Cor. 9:6 NIV)

This passage was applied to tithing—the idea was that we shouldn't look at it as taking away from the money that we have, but to look at it as sowing into God's Kingdom. And that when we sow, we will also reap. We are not just giving back to God, but we are also planting seeds for future blessings.

This was a new concept for us. We always gave out of duty in the past. Yes, we were glad to give (kind of) and yes, we gave willingly, but it was because that was what the Bible said to do—end of story. We didn't know that the principle behind giving was an "if/then" principle (like a mathematical equation; if x=5 and y=3 then x+y=8).

We thought that when we gave to God, that was the end of the story. But we began to realize that the Bible says, "IF a man sows generously, THEN he will also reap generously." This opened up a whole new realm for us.

Obviously, this was well different from the way we looked at life, so we were having a bit of trouble trying to implement it. When you change your entire way of looking at a particular subject, you have to reevaluate all of the beliefs that are attached to that subject.

One of the things that we really struggled with was, "How can we sow generously when we don't even have enough to meet our own bills?"

So, we would talk about it and not come to any definite conclusions, therefore our tithing fluctuated as widely as our finances. Don't get me wrong, we tithed, we were just having a very hard time getting this new way of looking at tithing through our thick skulls. If I were God, I would have been pretty frustrated with us!

One day, a couple of months after we had started to grapple with the concept of sowing and reaping, in the grand tradition of Christians across the nation, we decided to go out to dinner after church. Things had been so tight with our finances, we hadn't been out to eat in months. Before our money troubles, though, we would go out to eat once or twice a week, so we really missed it.

For what seemed like an eternity, we had given to the Lord first and had paid what bills we could, but we had no money left over for fun stuff like gas or groceries. Knowing this, we decided that the best thing to do that particular Sunday, was to spend what little money we had left at a restaurant. Pretty stupid, huh? Oh well, the Bible doesn't say that you have to be smart for God to love you. Good thing!

Well, we went to Pizza Hut. It is not my favorite place to eat, but we had young kids and we knew that they would do well there and would eat the food. (Read that last sentence carefully and you will understand why there are so many McDonalds in the world.)

We ordered a Supreme pizza and sat waiting for it. The kids drew on their placemats, the air was filled with the smell of grease and pepperoni, and life was tranquil. As we were waiting for our food, we saw some friends from church eating lunch. The little girl at the next table was in Caleb's Sunday School class. She was there with her mom or grandma and so we talked to them for a few minutes—just saying "Hi" and seeing how they were doing. Then God spoke.

We were back at our table and in my heart, I felt God say, "Pay for their lunch." I tried to ignore it. I responded; "Are you talking to me?" I thought maybe He had meant that conversation for someone else and it had gotten into my head by mistake. Maybe it was a batch email that I got but wasn't really meant for me. No such luck.

Did you ever notice how much harder it is to "hear God's voice" when we don't agree with what He says? Well, I certainly was having a difficult time hearing Him in this instance! I thought that maybe the problem was that He didn't understand our financial situation, so I explained it to Him again; "How in the world am I going to pay for their lunch? We have less than twenty dollars in our checking account, that's barely enough to pay for our own meal! There just isn't enough money to pay for their dinner, not to mention groceries for the rest of the week! I mean, come on, God, I know you understand the immutable laws of the cosmos, You made them! There is not enough money to pay for both lunches!"

"Pay for their lunch." He just wasn't budging on this whole issue, was He? I was starting to see that arguing with Him was an exercise in futility, so I took another tact. I put a set of conditions on my obedience that I was sure that He wouldn't be able to surmount. I would tell my wife what God had put on my heart and allow her to kibosh the idea. It had come down to a matter of obedience. Was I going to do what God wanted me to or was I going to follow my own path? Well, I would obey, but just to get in the last word, I said, "Fine, I'll do it, but you have to convince Pam!" That'll show Him, I thought.

Pam is the practical one in our relationship. She is the rudder of the ship. I am easily distracted by shiny objects, but she understands and accepts the limits of our current situation. I will be all excited about a new idea, come to her and say, "Hey, I've got a great way that we can make a ton of money! We will buy an emu farm in northern Africa, create a successful crossbreed between chicken and emu, ship them all over the world by rowboat, thereby solving all of the world's hunger problems and making a fortune simultaneously!" She looks at me with the lovingly patient eyes of a parent when presented with a frog for the fortieth time and says, "How much is that going to cost?" To which I reply; "Only 30-40 million dollars!" She gently brings me back to earth: "Do you have that much?" I, of course walk away grumbling, "Do I have that much? No, of course I don't have that much. That's why this would be a good venture…" You see, she is the one that grounds my ideas. Practical to a fault. I knew that she would do the same to this "flaky" idea from God.

Feeling a smug peace that my wife would tell God "what for," I leaned over to her and said; "I feel like God is saying that we are supposed to pay for those people's lunch." I sat back and waited for the sparks to ignite. No such luck. Pam looked back at me and said without hesitation; "OK." What a traitor—now the rug had been yanked out from under all of my arguments. Talk about an unsettled feeling!

All right! I know when I'm beaten. We called the waitress (or is the proper term "server" now?) over to our table. We informed her that we wanted to pay for our acquaintances' dinner. We asked her not to tell them who had squared their bill, just to let them know that someone had taken care of their dinner. She seemed kind of surprised and pleased to be part of this devious plot, so off she went to the kitchen to complete her secret agent-type duties.

Somehow the rest of our dinner tasted better, our conversation was lighter and our kids even seemed to be unusually well-behaved. (By saying well-behaved, I mean that no pepperoni ended up on the ceiling.) Of course this could all have been in my imagination. I knew that we had done what God wanted, though, and food always tastes better on a clean conscience. (There's a life lesson if I've ever heard one!)

We furtively watched out of the corners of our eyes as the waitress— sorry, "server" told the woman that their dinner was paid for. Her confusion brightened to a smile. She looked around the restaurant, hoping to catch the culprit, but anticipating this, we had already ducked our heads and pretended to be laughing at a prearranged joke. It worked, her eyes passed over us with nary a pause. She just shook her head with a bemused look as she and her lunch companion stood up and left the restaurant. As she walked past, though, I could see a grateful look sparkling in the corner of her eye. The sacrifice was worth it!

We finished the rest of our dinner and prepared to pay our bill. We weren't quite sure how we were going to do that, let alone how we were going to get through the rest of the week, but we knew that we had done what God had asked and were trusting Him to provide. We were packing up the leftover pizza to take home for later when the waitress came over to our table with a funny look on her face. We looked up expectantly and she placed a bill on the table and said, "This is the bill for the lunch that you bought for the people that just left—someone else picked up your tab."

We looked hard at her for a couple of minutes, fully expecting her to burst into laughter and tell us that it was all an elaborate joke, but she didn't. We looked at the bill and sure enough, it was much smaller than our tab was.

God spoke to my heart and said, "That is the principle of sowing and reaping. Because you sowed into someone else's life, I was able to pour out my blessings into your life. Instead of paying for dinner for four people, you paid for dinner for two people. You involved me in this situation through your giving and I made it work out in a better way than you could have even imagined."

Sowing and Reaping

Through this event, I finally understood sowing and reaping! Giving to God, whether time, energy or money was like investing. You are storing up blessings for later. It's not giving away money, never to be seen again. It is being smart about your finances.

There are a couple of principles about God's faithfulness in sowing and reaping that I learned through this experience.

1. What we sow, we will reap.
2. We involve God in our finances through giving.
3. He never lets us go without.

What we sow, we will reap

In farming, what you sow in the spring is what comes up in the summer. It is the same way with giving. The Bible says, "A man reaps what he sows." (Gal. 6:7 NIV) If you sow with a generous heart, you will reap great blessings. If you sow grudgingly, you will reap in the same manner. This is an easy truth to know in your head, but a hard truth to know in your heart.

Giving is a heart matter. One of the things that I noticed about the parable of the widow's mite is that the amount wasn't great to all outward appearances. I mean, the woman only gave two pennies, but because Jesus was able to look into the heart, he knew the spirit with which it was given. He understood that it was all the woman had, and that in giving this gift, she was saying to God that all her hopes, her dreams, her entire future rested in His hands alone.

It is much the same with giving. It is not enough to "give until it hurts." Your gift has to spring from a heart of thankfulness and love. Your heart has to be turned from a self-serving "gimme" heart and changed into a giving heart. In order to reap what you sow, you must sow with a heart of thanks and faith. When I give with the right motives and place myself in God's hands, He pours back to me in exponential measure!

We Involve God In Our Finances Through Giving

Malachi 3:10 says, "Bring the whole tithe into the storehouse, that there may be food in my house. Test me in this," says the Lord Almighty, "and see if I will not throw open the floodgates of heaven and pour out so much blessing that you will not have room enough for it. I will prevent pests from devouring your crops, and the vines in your fields will not cast their fruit," says the Lord Almighty. "Then all the nations will call you blessed, for yours will be a delightful land," says the Lord Almighty." (NIV)

This is an Old Testament scripture and some would say that we aren't held to it because Christ came. That's true—we are not held to the laws of the Old Testament anymore. This scripture, however, lays down a truth about how God deals with His people. The underlying theme is this: When we put God first monetarily, He will bless us. This does not mean that we will be millionaires or that we will have everything that our heart wants, but it does mean that we will be blessed—not just with direct repayment of what we have given to the Lord (money), but that he would protect our possessions, our families and other things. When we tithe, just like the widow who gave two pennies, we are putting our finances in God's hands. And God takes good care of His stuff.

God wants to bless us. He says in Proverbs 10:6, "Blessings crown the head of the righteous, but violence overwhelms the mouth of the wicked." (NIV) and in verse 22, "The blessing of the Lord brings wealth, and he adds no trouble to it." He really wants to bless us. Unfortunately for us, we have free will. God doesn't force Himself down our throats. He allows Himself to be limited to working in the areas that we give Him control.

When we tithe and give to God, that is the way that we give Him control in our finances. It opens the door for Him to pour out blessings in that area. It brings blessing.

God Never Lets us Go Without

One other thing that I learned about God's faithfulness that day: He will never let us go without. The Bible says, "I have never seen the righteous abandoned, or their children begging for bread." (Ps. 37:25 NIV) God does not leave us hanging. When we sow, we absolutely know that there will be a harvest! Of course we won't get everything we want, but He will make sure that we are provided for. Just like with my own children, I do my best to make sure that they have enough to eat, to wear, and a place to live, in the same way God makes sure that we have what we need.

That means when it is time to give of ourselves—our time, our energy, or even our money, we don't have to worry that we will somehow run out! If we trust God and do what He says, He will take care of the other details—like having enough food on the table. We came out of the "pizza incident" with enough money to get us through the week, buy groceries, gas, AND we got pizza. If we wouldn't have sown and done things God's way, we would have been very hungry that week.

God loves us very much. He wants what's best for us. That moment at Pizza Hut completely changed my heart and my perspective about giving and through it, God has blessed me again and again. And guess what? He's not above showering us with pizza in order to show us that we can trust Him.

Another Day

It was time for our second child. I'm not sure if we thought that our life was too calm, or we were in the beginning stages of psychosis. In truth, I think that the actual selling point was that we enjoyed the challenge of being parents! The sweet agony of pouring all of your logic into explaining why the laws of physics would not allow your three-year old to fly, only to have him jump off the top of the monkey bars just to prove you wrong was so enticing. (A note to all social services workers: That didn't actually happen. Really.) Something in us called out for more. Or maybe we just missed the smell of dirty diapers.

Hannah was different from Caleb right from the start. Pam, ever the glutton for punishment, decided that she would go by herself to Korea to pick up Hannah. (Did I explain that Hannah was adopted? Pam didn't just go and pick up some random child overseas.) Anyway, Pam planned on packing her bags, boarding a flight, sitting in a seat that is made to fit only half a person, flying across an ocean and landing in Korea a day later. Once there, she would try to communicate with people who spoke an entirely different language, find her hotel, and fall asleep at 8 a.m. because of the jet lag! The next day, she would meet our new daughter. This would be a wonderful time of emotional bonding for about two hours, after which she would go back to the hotel and sleep. The third day she was coming home. She would load a baby that she had met just the day before on an airplane and bond over a twenty-three hour flight!

I just have to say that my wife is an incredibly brave woman! I am very adventurous, and would have no qualms about parachuting out of an airplane, or bungee jumping, but there is absolutely no way I would ever consider the schedule that she had chosen to get Hannah!

She had done the same thing with Caleb, with a couple significant differences. She had a friend along and they shared the responsibility of keeping him calm and quiet. They stayed in Korea for about seven days and were able to see Caleb every day and get to know him. They acclimated to the time difference and weren't sleep deprived. Even with all of these advantages though, it was a hard trip home with him. Caleb never stopped wiggling. He made his feelings of unhappiness known to everyone on the plane. Needless to say, I was thinking of having Pam's head examined for wanting to go through the experience again—by herself.

All of my worry was for naught, though, because the trip home with Hannah was different. It was calm. It was quiet. Hannah didn't wiggle. She was content to cuddle in Pam's arms and sleep—the whole trip. It was as if she was the most laid back baby in the world, constantly listening to relaxation tapes. I should have realized right then that we were dealing with a whole different type of child!

Boy, was Hannah different than Caleb! She was smiley, he was somber. He was spicy, she was sweet. She was still, he never stopped moving. He was as skinny as a rail, she had rolls of baby fat. He was boisterous, she was quiet. He was independent, she was completely dependent.

We brought her home and set her in the middle of the floor on a blanket and waited for her to do something. She didn't. She just sat there. If we would have done the same thing with Caleb at that age, within five minutes he would have disassembled the VCR and reprogrammed the remote control. She just sat there. It wasn't that Hannah was lazy, she was just content.

Fast forward to present day Hannah. She is beautiful—of course, I may be biased because she's my daughter. She has an angelic face with cheeks that just beg to be kissed. She has hair the color of coal but with a shine like diamonds. In fact every bit of who she is shines. It's like there is a glow that comes from somewhere deep inside of her and when she cuddles up next to you, you feel somehow illuminated.

You see, Hannah never has a bad day. Every single situation she comes up against, she tackles with a smile. She truly believes that each person that she meets will love her, and they do. She refers to every single man, woman and child in the entire western hemisphere as her friend, and will take you by the hand to go play with "her friends"—that she's just met.

Her spirit is irrepressible. That doesn't mean that she doesn't get into trouble. She does. But she handles it different than our son. If you tell Caleb "No," and he has it in his mind to disobey, he will get a nasty look on his face, storm off to his room and pout. She, on the other hand, will look at you, smile and do the thing that you have just told her not to do.

She is just as strong-willed as our son. They both want things their way and make no bones about it, they just tackle the issue with a different game plan. Hannah employs a tactic that I like to call "passive defiance." She pours on the charm, bats her eyelashes and does whatever she pleases anyway. The problem is, by the time that you, as the parent realize that you have been conned, too much time has passed for the consequence of her actions to make much difference. I think when she gets older, she may become a spy and engage in covert ordnance tactics!

Hannah is not by any means a naughty child. She is a genuinely sweet, happy girl. Every single time I walk in the door from my workday, no matter how bad the day has been, no matter how many times she has gotten in trouble that day, she runs at me like a Mongol horde yelling, "Daddy, daddy, daddy, daddy!" She tackles me with the force of a linebacker and attaches herself to my lower extremities.

No matter what has gone on during my day, no matter who yelled at me, no matter how bad my day was, I feel like a hero. Everything changes in that instant. The past, the junk just doesn't even matter. In that moment, I know that anything is possible—that the disappointments of the day don't have power anymore.

When she was younger and still in her crib, she would be up before us every single morning. It was as if her internal clock was set for six-thirty in the morning. We liked to sleep in until about eight, so she was always up before us. Her room had pastel green carpeting, and white furniture. The sun would strain through her window blinds and kiss her face with an early morning blessing. And then, she would wake up.

She never made a fuss, though. She would just lay in her crib and when I came into the room, and opened the shades, she would be looking up at me from her bed with a big smile on her face as if to say, "I knew you would come and get me. I knew that you would be here to help me greet the day. I am so excited about the things that we are going to experience together today!"

That attitude made everything feel right. At the time, our family was going through a really rough time. We didn't have the money we needed to make the bills, we were going in the hole financially, and things were very stressful for both Pam and I at work. We were feeling defeated and demoralized. People that we thought we could trust were spreading lies and rumors about us. On top of all that other stuff, our church was in turmoil and it didn't look like it was going to pull out any time soon. We had been in this situation for so long, it didn't feel like there was any end in sight. But in that time of see-sawing on the waves of emotion, in the time when everything looked not dark and stormy, but drab and dreary, in the time of hopelessness, Hannah's attitude each morning was the one spark of hope.

I realized that no matter what horrid things were going on around us, and no matter how bleak the future looked, it didn't matter to her. She was content that there was a new day. She was excited for what the new day offered, and she was glad that we would be able to share those experiences together.

I realized that there was a lesson about God's faithfulness in her attitude. I was being overwhelmed by my problems. He, through Hannah was reminding me that each day is a fresh start. That with Him, all things are new. I was allowing my expectations of the future to drag me down (I was expecting things to continue to get worse, or stay as bad as they were). He was showing me that I could choose to believe in His greatness. That I could choose to believe that He was going to make things better.

The funny thing was, once I adopted the attitude that each new day held promise and not disappointment, things began to get better. The change didn't happen overnight, I had to subsist on faith for quite a while, but within a year I had a new job while the business built back up, Pam was able to work less hours outside the home, and we were able to buy a beautiful new home. And it all started because Hannah taught me that each new day was filled with new possibilities.

I thought about what that meant for my life, and sat down and wrote this song:

ANOTHER DAY

You greet the day with a smile
Hidden right behind your eyes
And in that glimpse of eternity
I smile too
Cause there's something about you
That opens possibilities

Another day another time
Another chance to blow my mind
The story isn't done
The tellling's just begun
Another day another song
One more chance to right my wrong
Another chance to know
Everything is gonna be fine

You know, I've found no matter what the situation, how bad things look, what I am going through, what others have said about me, or how I've messed up, when I trust in God, I can face the new day with a smile and truly say, "Everything is gonna be fine."

Trusting in Another Day

Hannah's personality has taught me about trust in God's faithfulness. She has taught me about the importance of having unwavering belief in His ability to handle all of my junk—my impossible situations, my emotional tirades, my human frailties. With God, every single day is a new chance. Another chance for Him to blow our mind with His amazing presence. Another chance for us to experience His love, His grace, His truth. The past has been wiped away. Yes, we still have to pay the consequences of our bad decisions, but as the Bible says, "Because of the Lord's great love we are not consumed, for his compassions never fail. They are new every morning; great is your faithfulness." (Lamentations 3: 22-23 NIV)

It is so easy to say "His mercies are new every morning," but have you ever thought about what that really means? How would it change your life if every morning when you woke up, no matter how bad the day was before, you had the expectation sown deep inside you that today God had some great things planned; that today was a day that God could completely change your bad situation, or blow your mind with the greatness of His plan for you?

What if, the day after you got fired from your job, you sat up in bed and had the belief cemented in you like a cornerstone that God had something great for you today? That the next job was just around the corner? That His plans for your life are better than you can even imagine? How would you live that day differently than if you allowed yourself to wallow in self-pity? What chances would you take that you wouldn't otherwise? What would the results of your changed attitude have on your life?

It's been said that people who expect good things, usually receive them and people that look for bad things usually find them. If we look at each new day as an opportunity for God's greatness to show itself, if we have unwavering trust in the faithfulness of God, and if we expect God to be faithful to the promises that He has given us in the Bible, namely that He has a plan for us, a good plan, a couple of things happen. The first is that our troubles don't seem so overwhelming, and the second thing that happens is that we are much more able to move forward with our lives and aren't laid out flat every time Satan knocks us down.

A lot of times I get caught up in the difficulty and internal wranglings of the situation and forget the long view. It's so easy to get your head turned around and find yourself fretting over the fact that things look drastic right now. And they may be drastic at this moment. The problem may be that there isn't enough money for the mortgage, or your child is doing poorly in school, your job is overwhelming, or your marriage is headed for divorce. These are big problems. If you focus on them, they will drive you mad. I am not telling you to bury your head in the sand and things will get better. That would be stupid.

By all means, you should do all you can to solve the problems—get another job, see a counselor, or help your child study, but the flip side of the coin is that we need to trust God that He will work things out in the best way possible. When you reach the end of what you can do, then you have to believe in "another day."

I have found that when I focus my attention on God, the problems seem much smaller. This is the God that created the galaxies by the power of his words! This is the God that took a rib from a man and made a woman. This is the God that knows the end from the beginning, that "brings the dead to life and calls the things that are not as though they were." (Rom. 9:17 NIV) Do you really think that anything is too difficult for Him?

Trust and hope. That is what God brings to life. When we trust in our strength, it fails us. When we hope in the world's system, it breaks us. But, when we trust Him and put the difficult situations in His hands, He works them to our benefit.

After the flood, God placed a rainbow in the sky as a sign to Noah that He would never flood the entire earth again. But it was more than that. It was the sign of a new beginning. And each and every day that we get up, the fact that the sun rises in the sky is a sign to us that today is a new beginning! The old has passed away and the new has come. The mistakes that you made yesterday are forgiven. Your sins are washed away. Take new steps. In faith. Don't be afraid to try something new, to look like a fool, to fail or succeed!

When you have the view that God is ultimately trustworthy and that through Him each and every day is new, you begin to look at the world in a different manner. You look at the potential of success instead of the fear of failure. There is a verse in the Bible that reads "With man this is impossible, but with God all things are possible." (Mt. 19:26 NIV) Why? Aside from the fact that God is much more powerful and wise that we are, man limits himself. We let our view of what is possible or impossible cloud our vision and determine our course of action.

We must have the hope of another day! We have to trust that the sun rising today means that we have another chance to be what God called us to be! It is imperative for us to believe to the core of our spirit that this is not the end, but the beginning—that today could be the day that God will totally blow our mind with the greatness of His presence! We have to expect that God is perched on the edge of His throne, waiting with bated breath to move on our behalf! It is this knowledge that changes us, that makes us unafraid, that shows us His greatness and beauty. It is this belief in another day, another chance, that makes all the difference!

strange Changes

There is a poem by Robert Frost that starts out "Two roads diverged in a yellow wood…" He uses this as a metaphor for life and the choices that we make. As he describes the different paths, you can see that it makes a great deal of difference which one he chooses. The poem ends with these words: "Two roads diverged in a wood, and I, I took the one less traveled by."

The road of faith is truly the road less traveled by. It is immensely uncomfortable. Many times you don't know where you are going. There are mountainous rocks that block your path. Sometimes, you stand there, a look of profound bewilderment on your face while flies circle your head; you imagine you see the buzzards waiting for their next meal and you wonder what in the world to do next. But the road of faith is the only one worth traveling. It is the only path that reaches the summit.

Our cute, comfortable lives had taken a nosedive. The business that I had started had plummeted. I had not gotten paid a dime in over six months. We were burning through our cash reserves at an alarming rate. Pam was tense and anxious because of finances and the need for her to work more hours. And just when we thought it couldn't get worse, some major problems surfaced at our church.

Understand that we had been at the church for over 12 years. We loved and were loved by these people. I was the worship leader, Pam was the nursery coordinator. We had grown into these positions through the nurturing of this church. This is where we had discovered the joy of serving God.

In college, the Christian campus group we were a part of was anchored to the church and so it was the most natural progression that when we were married and graduated from college that we made it our church home.

As in all small churches, we made deep friendships that lasted a long time. Now, though, it seemed we had come to a divergence in our paths. We looked at where we wanted to go in our Christianity and we looked at the direction that the church was taking, and we knew that they were two different ways. It was a heart-rending realization that in itself would have been worse than gall bladder surgery, but when it jumped on top of the pile of other manure-like things that had happened, it was just unbearable.

We felt as if we had reached the sludge that is beneath the slime that was under the murky depths of a swampy pond. There was no going any lower. I was at this place with a fifty to sixty hour-a-week job that incidentally, I didn't get paid for. My wife was on the verge of a nervous breakdown. Our retirement was spent, and the church that we had been a part of for so many years had imploded. We had about as much hope as Arnold Schwarzenegger had of becoming Governor of California. (Wait a minute, didn't that happen? Bad example.)

One bright spot in the midst of all of this was that despite all the nastiness, our family was strong and happy. We had two wonderful kids, and every day, Pam and I grew closer together. Of course, it's hard not to be close when you're always apologizing to each other because of the fights you had gotten into over money, stress and life in general.

Even though we were doing well as a family, I was despondent. I had this deep-seated, gnawing feeling that things were bad, but don't worry, tomorrow, they might get worse! My life had become rare moments of sunshine smiles in the otherwise darkening twilight of hopelessness.

I asked myself, "Why are you so unhappy?" It seemed like an obvious question, but I really wasn't aiming for the sublime here, folks. My answer flashed quickly and hurtfully. "Because you are a complete and utter failure." Well, I thought I was being a little harsh with myself, but as I pondered it a bit more, as I really probed how I felt about myself, that was the only thing that rang with honesty. I felt like a complete failure.

There is a certain freedom that comes from being a hopeless failure. I'm not saying that you should try it at your earliest convenience, but think about it: there is no way that you can sink any lower. All the plans and aspirations that you had about your ability to do things on your own strength, to be the "hero" are splintered and there is only one way to go. Up. I imagine it's kind of like the way the prodigal son might have felt when he woke up with the pigs, looked around and said "Hey, I'm in a pig sty." Again, not a real astute observation, but his brain was probably addled by the smell.

"Why do I feel this way?" I asked myself. "I am supposed to be this family's provider." I answered. Well, for six months, I have not only provided nothing, but I have taken away from our reserves. "I am supposed to be a good Christian." I thought. But ever since I laid someone off because of budget cutbacks from the business, they have done nothing but cause trouble and spread vicious lies about me. My wife is having to work much more that she should have to and the strain was beginning to show around her eyes. I couldn't even get my kids Christmas presents this past holiday! Of course I was depressed!

I went out for a walk to clear my thoughts, or as I might more accurately put it, to complain to God. As I stepped outside my door, the bite of the cold took my breath away. We lived on a dirt road five miles from the nearest light. If you listened carefully, you could hear the lowing of the beefalo across the pasture, and every four or five days a car would drive by. Embellishment aside, it was peaceful and serene.

On this clear night, the stars hung like pinhole lights in the sky and the moon was so bright, it cast shadows on the ground. The road was straight and the tire tracks made two glowing paths of promise in the foot-deep snow. The crunch of my boots in the snow was the only sound as the rest of the world fell into a reverent silence. I knew that God was getting ready to speak.

I decided it was the best idea to stop my complaining and listen to what He wanted to tell me. I find that it is much easier to listen when the sound isn't confused with my own aimless mutterings. When God speaks to me, I have yet to hear an audible voice, but it is as if thoughts come into my head and I know they are God's. And that is what happened that clear night. He said, "I love you." Those three words alone brought tears to my eyes, the power and strength behind them forced away all feelings of failure. With three words, God banished my inadequacies and let me dare to believe that I was loveable. It wasn't as if, magically, I no longer felt like a failure, but the poison was no longer in the arrow. I was loved, and the words were accompanied by such a strong surge of emotion that I knew that it wasn't just lip service.

In my finite mind, that would have been enough, but God wasn't done yet. He had only brought me to a place where I could hear and believe the next part of His words to me: "I am getting ready to move you. I will move you into a new job. I will pick you up like the children of Israel and move you to a new land." Now, if I were really holy, He probably would have ended with "Thus saith the Lord." And illuminated the night sky with cerulean for several minutes. Unfortunately, I guess I'm not that holy, so that was all I got. But, it was enough.

I responded in the only way that one can respond to a visit from the Creator of the Heavens—I said, "Thanks." Honestly, I was too overwhelmed to respond in any other way. Then I waited. I guess I was thinking that He would move me at that moment. Or maybe I was hoping that He would; I mean Peter was moved from one place to another in the Bible, I'm sure that God could do it again.

After several minutes of standing in the snow, I decided that I should probably clarify my position to God, just in case He misunderstood. I told Him I was ready to go. Now. And then again, like a good child of God, I waited.

I waited for a day. Then, I waited for a week. A month. Three months. I began to get anxious. Maybe I misheard God. Maybe I missed the opportunity. Four months. Things kept getting worse. Five months. We had absolutely no money whatsoever. We had depleted all of our savings and retirement. We were still several thousand short each month. It was a rather disturbing situation.

During this time, the one bright spot in our existence was that we found the church that we could call home. We began to get involved. Somehow, they found out that I was a worship leader and so I began to lead worship. It was a breath of fresh air. We were challenged. We were growing. We started to make connections. Then the pastor quit.

Truth be told, the pastor was following God's plan. He felt God had sent him to the church for a season and that the season was done. We saw that, but more deeply, we began to wonder if there was something wrong with us. This was the second pastor to leave in six months! Rather unnerving!

We knew we were called to the church, though and not the pastor, so we stayed. (Did that sound overly religious? If so, I apologize.) In any event, another pastor came in and we began to bond with him. It was well with us.

Six months. Seven months, eight months—nothing. Things were getting better, but not really, if you know what I mean. We still had no money, our reserves had been depleted for so long they were but a fond memory, like the remembrance of a day at the beach in the middle of winter. Our faith was increasing, but in our incredibly deep, profound, seek-God-till-you-drop way (notice the sarcasm?) we were tired of just growing spiritually!

It's amazing how shallow you can seem once you put your true thoughts down on paper, but you wanted honesty—well, there it is. We were sick of our situation! Tired of trying to decide whether we should buy milk or gas the next week. We just didn't want to have to explain to our kids again why they weren't getting Christmas presents.

Neither of us said it out loud, but I thought: "We're smart people with great earning potential! Pam has a job where she could earn almost six figures if she worked full time, I could earn about that much too if things were going better. What in the world is going on? What are we doing?"

As I thought along those lines, the temptation was great to make some changes and look for an escape. God said that He was going to move us, right? There's nothing wrong with helping Him along a little bit, is there? We could look for some way to provide for ourselves; we could make things happen for ourselves. I was just tired of waiting for God. I just wasn't entirely sure that He hadn't gotten sidetracked and forgotten all about our situation!

Of course we both knew that taking it upon ourselves to make those changes would be wrong. We would not be trusting in God to provide, it would be our "Ishmael." And just like the story of Abraham in the Bible, we wouldn't acquire anything but trouble by doing it.

Pam had to continue working part time. I had to continue working at the business. We had to continue to trust God to bring in every peso, yen, penny, and euro that we could use to buy our pitiful allotment of groceries!

This went on and on, and I began to understand the meaning of the fact that God is eternal. He has no beginning, and I was starting to think that this situation had no end!

At the peak of my frustration, I went for a walk. It was a clear night again and I began to pour out my frustrations. God listened out of politeness for a few moments and then silenced me. Even I know that when the person with enough power to create the entire universe in six days with the power of His words tells you to be quiet, you'd better be absolutely still! So, I stood there. Silent. Listening.

Then, in my mind, I saw huge pieces—as big a continents being moved across the night sky. There were hundreds of them. They moved very slowly and as they moved, the heavens groaned and rumbled like the sound of dragging an immense weight over gravel. Many pieces were in place, and others were moving into their proper fit. And as they moved, I somehow knew the effort it took to push them even one inch off their original resting place. I saw that they all fit together, but it was impossible to move them quickly, so intricate was the puzzle. Some pieces had to be in place before another piece could even be moved. Others had to be taken out to make room for the right piece to take its place. I somehow knew that this was my life. That these were the pieces of my life that were still to be written. I knew that the effort that it took to move those situations, people, jobs, and money into place was immense.

Then God spoke to my heart. "This is what I am doing on your behalf. Be patient. These pieces must all be in place before visible change can occur. Understand that I am moving. And when the puzzle is complete, it will happen. And you will know it is me."

A complete peace surrounded me. I had seen the situation through God's eyes and it gave me hope for the future. Things continued on unchanged on the surface, but I was content.

About a month later, I got a call from a pastor across the state. I went to meet with him as a favor to a friend, and he offered me a job—as a pastor! The one thing I never wanted to be. As Pam and I talked about it though, we realized that this was the move that God had worked so hard to orchestrate for us. And like Abraham, when God told him to go to the land that God would show him, we began to pack. So much for me even being able to guess at the mind of God!

God's Puzzle Pieces

The thing that struck me the most as I was going through this situation is the fact that God puts together puzzle pieces on our behalf. He puts considerable effort and time into making sure every piece is in the right place at the right time. That thought alone blew me away—the almighty creator of the earth puts forward more that just a passing effort in order to make sure my life works out as planned! As I considered it more, though, I realized that His great care for me really came as no surprise.

You see, you and I are God's children. I thought about my kids and I realized that I would do almost anything in the world to make sure that they turned out well. And guess, what? God's feelings toward us are very much the same. The only difference is that He has many more resources than we do to make that happen. No matter how hard I tried, if my son asked me to make the sun stand still to prove the truth of my words to him, I couldn't. I would try my hardest, but just end up with a headache from concentrating. The difference? God can—and has (check out the story of Joshua in Joshua 10:7-14!)

God will move the heavens on your behalf when you follow His will! God will make the sun stand still if it will prove to you His love for you.

That's why it says in the Bible that "in all things God works for the good of those who love Him, who have been called according to His purpose." (Rom. 8:28 NIV) Bad things happen. God does not bring them to you, but He is moving puzzle pieces. He knows the end from the beginning. He sees the big picture. All He asks is that you trust Him and follow Him with all of your heart and soul and strength.

If you had a friend that could see the future, who had proven that ability time after time, and he told you to invest in a particular company, what would you do? I don't know about you, but I would sell everything, even the shirt off my own back in order to get as much money as I could to put it into this company. Why? Three reasons: number one, this friend wants the best for me, number two, he has information that I don't have, and finally, he has proven himself trustworthy.

Why would it be any different with God? Those same three reasons are true for Him as well, only more so. He wants what is best for you. In fact God wants what's best for you so much, that He allowed His only son to degrade, denigrate, and humiliate himself by coming to earth and dying for you—all this while you still hated Him! Have you truly grasped the depth of His care for you? I still struggle to accept it.

The second reason that it's a really good idea to follow God's plan is this: He has information that we don't have. I mean think about it! He created the entire cosmos with the words of His mouth! I can't bring anything into existence by commanding it to appear! Believe me, I've tried! "I speak unto you, brussel sprouts and command you to become steak!" See, nothing. Obviously God knows things that we don't. It says in the Bible that God knows the end from the beginning. Do you know what that means? (Say this with a stage whisper.) He can tell the future!

The final reason is this: He has proven Himself trustworthy. Even if your own life seems short on incidents where God has been worthy of your trust, look at the Bible. See how God was faithful to Joseph, to Noah, to Mary and so many others. If you allow Him, He'll prove Himself faithful to you too.

God is always moving those gigantic puzzle pieces into place in your life. I challenge you to have the courage to follow His path. In my situation, if all of the things that had gone wrong hadn't, I wouldn't have wanted to move. If we hadn't had to trust God intimately for every single penny, we would have never understood how trustworthy He was. And if I wouldn't have felt God moving in my heart with a Holy Discontent in my present job situation, I NEVER would have become a pastor.

The path of faith is hard sometimes, but in all things, whether good or bad, remember, it is just a piece of the puzzle.

Hunting a House

Ever since I was a young child growing up on the "mean streets" of suburbia, walking past the "gangs" in the halls of my parochial school, (in reality, they were probably just groups of people talking about the latest basketball game), I have had but one aim in life. Not to be a pastor.

I had nothing against pastors, my dad was one. I just really didn't want to be one. It's a great profession/calling. A good pastor has the right words to say to make you want to grow spiritually, and you never doubt their care about your personal situation. Maybe I just didn't think I had it in me. Maybe I was disenchanted by what I considered to be inconsistencies in Christians, or maybe I was just scared. All things considered, I'm not sure where my love for not pastoring came from, but there it was nonetheless.

I grew up in the church. It was great. I was the son of the pastor. We got a ham around Easter time, and there were always plenty of grandmother-types running around with lint-covered mints in their pockets for deserving boys and girls. There were Christmas plays, musicals, cantatas, liturgies, home visits, board meetings, Easter sunrise service, long hours, overwork, exhaustion, disenfranchisement... and the list goes on.

Actually, nothing really horrible happened to my dad as a result of being in the ministry, other than the unfortunate side effect of him being pretty non-existent during my formative years. I'm not sure where this desire to not be a pastor came from, whether it was a backlash against what my dad went through, or if it just didn't fit into my image of myself. Well, for whatever reason, the end result was a boy whose every prayer sounded something like this: "Thank you, God, for all You've done, and for mommy and daddy... andletmepleasenotbeapastorthanks."

As I explained in the previous chapter, I had received a call to be a pastor. It would require me to move across the state. No problem. I would be paid a reasonable salary. Definitely no problem. I would be able to continue to run the business that I had started, one day a week. Not at all a problem. I would get to work with the arts. No problem. I would have to be a pastor. Big problem!

So, there I was, with an extra helping of pastoring on my plate and a decision to make. Was I going to eat it or not? The job I had just been offered was as a creative arts pastor for a church. Would I accept it? Would I give up on my lifelong dream of not being a pastor? (Here is where the dramatic music will go in the movie version of my life; "A Perfect Whiner—The Ben Eggers Story.)

I prayed about it. God answered. He said, "Yes, take the job." I didn't like His answer. So, I had Pam pray about it. God didn't change his mind. Drat! I broached the subject with the kids. They had the audacity to be excited about the change! I was just getting nowhere with my protest! It was crystal clear that this was the direction that He had for us. I figured I needed to get used to it.

So God wanted me to be a pastor. This was the seven-lane freeway he had marked out for my family. Great. I thought maybe it was just the title "pastor" that carried the stigma, so I implored the senior pastor to bestow another title on me, such as "Head of the Arts Department," or "Creative Arts Associate." I was even open to being titled "Despot in Charge of all Things Art-Related." It was to no avail. The pastor gave me a speech about the honor in being a pastor and accepting the title complete with scripture references. Aaaaarrrrrggg!

Once I got over my little hissy fit about being a pastor, though, I was rather excited about this job direction. The type of things that I would be doing were things that I had loved and been training for my whole life—drama, music… the arts.

Ever since I was tiny enough to fit in my mother's palm, (well, maybe not that small), I had been involved in the arts. I was in choir, barbershop octet, plays, musicals, river dancing… I didn't really do river dancing, but it really sounded impressive didn't it? Suffice to say, this job was right down my alley.

But just like most people in similar situations, I wanted to make sure that I had heard the Lord correctly, so Pam and I decided that we would go and check out the church and the area. I guess I figured, if it was good enough for the children of Israel, it was good enough for me. So we made plans to visit the area for a couple of days.

On a lark, we contacted a realtor in the area and set up a couple of house showings. I didn't really expect to find anything, but I did want to get a feel of the housing market in the area. Maybe some small part of me was hoping that we would look at some houses, hate them and call the whole thing off.

Really, I just wanted to find a house that was bigger than the one we had at the time. You see, the land we currently lived on was stunning. We had twenty rolling acres with two ponds, a meadow area, over fifty apple trees and a wooded creek. It was the type of place where you would expect elves and rabbits to live side-by-side. I spent many quiet hours sitting by one of the ponds and listening to the katydids sing their sad, sweet song as the sun set over the water. We had bought the house for the land.

Our house, on the other hand, left a lot to be desired—about 1500 square feet. It was only 1100 square feet with tiny rooms. Now before you decry me for wanton greed because our house was bigger than yours and here I am crying in my soup for more room, you have to understand something. We had moved from a house with 2700 square feet, four bedrooms, three bathrooms, and only one child to a place barely over one-third the size and just for kicks, added another child!

Don't get me wrong, I'm all for closeness in a family. I tend to desire emotional closeness, though, rather than physical closeness. I find that for myself, too much of the second gets in the way of the first. In order for me to function well, I need to be able to escape. To find a place to be alone. To process my thoughts. It is rather hard to do, though, when your entire house, except for the bedrooms and bathroom consists of one room, most of which is taken up by the plethora of toys my wonderful children had stored in the middle of the walkways.

I'd like to say that I just hung out in the bathroom when I needed to be alone, but that was small enough that if you wanted to dry off after your shower, all you would have to do is hang towels on the walls and turn around a few times. It just didn't work. There was no escape. The situation sometimes made for a very grumpy daddy.

Our intention, when we purchased the home was to fix it up, sell it in a year and build another, larger home on the other part of the property. It had been two years, though, and there was no chance of building in sight, so, needless to say, I was ready to commit hara-kiri just to have a moment of blessed peace!

All that to say, I guess when we set up the house viewings, I wasn't asking for much. I was just hoping for a house that was a little bit bigger than the one we had at the time.

The day arrived that we were going to check out the church. We went to the service and really felt like we belonged. The people were friendly, the services upbeat, and there was enormous potential there. We took a drive around the area and were greeted by beaches and trees along with a small town closeness offset by the nearness of malls and restaurants that we craved. Perfect.

All was not flawless, though. During the course of our visit with people and in listening to the stories of their troubles in finding a home, we came to the conclusion that maybe we should find a house that was a bit more of a starter-type and then build in a couple of years. It seemed that many of our new friends had struggled long and hard to find a suitable residence, and so I was not all that hopeful about our chances.

With this in mind, we thought that the only way to get what we wanted in a home was to build. I'm not sure why this was an appealing idea to me seeing as I had done three huge remodeling projects in the past two years. But I guess that's the type of thing that doesn't look as bad as a lobotomy, but when you're in the middle of it, you wish you would have had the lobotomy instead.

As we came back to the hotel in the afternoon for our Sunday afternoon nap, before sleep overtook us, we felt peace at the direction God had given us. We would take the new job, I would give up my feeble protest about being a pastor. We would move to the area and buy a starter home. After a year, we would start building something that we would love. After all, we had just lived in a tiny house with two kids driving us out of our minds all eleven months of winter, how bad could it be?

We woke up and went to meet the real estate agent. On the way, Pam told me that she had prayed that we would find our house that day. I outwardly encouraged her, told her that God had His hand in it, and stood in faith with her. Inside, I said, "Yeah right! We're only looking at four houses today!" I'm such a hypocrite, aren't I? Shhh, don't tell anyone!

The houses we were going to view were split evenly in type. Two of them would fit the bill of more of a starter home and two were pie-in-the-sky if we inherited one million dollars tomorrow, we MIGHT be able to afford them. Actually, they were only about $80,000 more than the other houses, but that wasn't the direction we had decided we were heading in, so we were only looking at them to be polite.

The first house was a huge white monstrosity set on the end of a cul-de-sac. The interior was painted in the daring color white and seemed very small for such a large house. It protruded three stories into the sky and had a living room that was bigger vertically than horizontally. It was great, but it was not for us.

The second and third houses were more along the lines of what we were looking for. They were in the starter home price range. They were new construction. They were cute, but they were still a little small. That's OK, we could live with that. This was definitely the way to go. We decided when we came back to the area to seriously look at homes, we would focus more on this type of home and find something that would be ideal for us.

Then we drove up to the last house. It was perfect. It had a beautiful white front porch, a spacious two car garage, and an extra thirty-by-forty foot garage to the side. The siding was tan with white trim work. The generous-sized windows invited us inside. The beautifully manicured lawn and flowerbeds beckoned to us. It was large, but had just the right amount of charm to make it look homey.

We walked in. Fourteen-foot ceilings soared above us, warm hard-wood floors greeted our feet, and there was a fireplace! We went downstairs to a fully finished basement complete with a family room, guest room, guest bathroom, and playroom where the kids could keep all their junk! (I mean precious toys.) I was in heaven! The house was easily three-and-a-half times bigger than our old house without being obnoxious.

Then we saw the kid's bedrooms. We had two children, Caleb, seven years old and Hannah, two years old. There were two children's bedrooms. The boy's bedroom was painted blue and red with car decorations. It even had a car faceplate on the light switch. The girl's room was decorated in pale green. There was a swing that hung from the ceiling, and one whole wall was painted with a mural of a white picket fence and bees and butterflies buzzing about. It was as if the mother ship had called Hannah home! These were her favorite things.

I knew we were in trouble. We walked into the master bedroom and our mouths became caves that flies could explore with freedom, we were so stunned! There was a master bathroom with a walk-in closet, a garden tub, a shower and two sinks! And there was something off to the side of that room that was a secret desire of ours but we had never told anyone. Behind two French glass doors stood the perfect library!

We were flabbergasted. We found out that the previous owners had built the house for themselves, then his job transferred him. It was as if God had read all of our innermost desires, had someone build this house for us, decorate it, and move away after being in the house for less than six months, just so that we could have it! The best part was that the house was priced about $15,000 under market value!

I was a little concerned about whether or not the bank would approve the loan, but I figured that if God wanted us to have this home, He would work it out. I told the real estate agent that he wouldn't hear from us for about a month, after which we would call and buy the house. And that's exactly what happened.

God Wants to Bless Us

The other day, I saw a shirt that said, "My body will only do what my mind tells it that it can." It's the same thing with blessings in our lives. Through this experience, I realize that too often, I limit the blessings God wants to bring in my life. My mind won't allow the blessings to be bigger than I think they should be. God wants to bless us more than what our pitiful imaginations can come up with, though. I Corinthians 2:9 says, "…No eye has see, no ear has heard, no mind has conceived what God has prepared for those who love Him." (NIV)

Our God is an extravagant God. A lot of times, unfortunately, I make Him into a small God. I accept a small blessing and consider that to be the best that He can do. All the while, He wants to give me a much bigger blessing! It's like a child that goes to the toy store with their mom or dad. The parent tells the child, "Pick out anything you want. I have a huge amount of money and I want to buy something for you. I love you and want to bless you!" The child looks at all the colorful toys with wide eyes, the iPods, the bikes, the radio controlled cars, the Playstations. He touches the action figures, swings on the swing sets, then goes to the checkout counter, and chooses as his gift a piece of gum from the vending machine near the checkout.

God has no limits. Job 11: 7-8 says, "Can you fathom the mysteries of God? Can you probe the limits of the Almighty? They are higher than the heavens—what can you do? They are deeper than the depths of the grave—what can you know?" (NIV)

If God is limitless, and He wants to bless us, why do we settle for the piece of gum when He wants to give us the radio-controlled car? We put the limits on Him. Many times we choose the small gift, the small blessing because we just can't make ourselves believe in a God that is limit-less!

There's a scene in the movie "The Matrix" where Morpheus is train-ing Neo on how to bend the rules of the Matrix, a computer program that has controlled humanity for many years. They are standing on the rooftop of a fifty-story building, where Morpheus is explaining that your mind has to believe in the impossible. Then he looks Neo in the eye and says "Free your mind." He turns and runs to the edge of the roof and leaps into the air, soaring an impossible 100 yards before landing on the rooftop across the street, the impact making a depression in the roof!

We, too need to free our minds! In order to do that, we must believe two things: first, that God wants to bless us extravagantly. Second, that God can do the impossible. We should expect that God wants to provide abundantly for us.

Don't get me wrong, we can't have anything we want. But we also don't have to feel guilty because we are the son or daughter of a very rich and extravagant King that loves to do things for His children.

For example, take the house that God provided for us. It was way above what we thought we could afford. It had everything that we wanted in a house. It even had a library—something that we had dreamed about, but never had on our list of things to look for in a home. It had a playroom for the kids, a family room as well as a living room. It even had high ceilings, something that I had been yearning for ever since moving into our previous seven-foot ceiling house. God took every desire of our hearts and put it into that house. The whole thing was too good to be true, but God provided a way for us to be blessed with it. He gave it to us as a gift.

The house that God blessed us with is a testament to His greatness, not our own. The thing is, we didn't have to accept it. We could have lim-ited our blessing to a lesser house. We could have been overwhelmed with guilt that we didn't deserve such a nice house; we didn't deserve God's blessing. We could have allowed our shame at having something like that to take over. But instead we chose to believe in a God that delights in blessing His children.

What kind of God do you believe in? Do you believe that as God's son or daughter that God wants to bless you? Or are you just eking out existence with stingy blessings? Do you believe for great things, not just monetarily, but in your relationships, your job, your emotional well-being? Do you believe that you deserve happiness? Or are you wracked with guilt and eschew true blessings because you feel unworthy of happiness?

Please remember, God wants to bless you! His resources are unlimited. He wants you to have peace, He wants to show His greatness in your life. Just like any parent delights in giving their child a gift and seeing that child's exhilaration when they open the package, in the same way, God wants to see your face as he showers you with gifts of love! The only question that remains is this: will you accept His blessings?

To Sell or Not to Sell

You know, the end of our plan is never the end of THE plan, especially when you are following God's plan. How did you like that incredibly confusing sentence? Notice how many times I used the word "plan"? It's OK, you can be impressed. Anyway, there we were, God had moved us to a totally new job, thereby giving us a steady source of income. He had confirmed this direction several times, He had shown us the house that we were supposed to buy and we were excited.

There was just one problem. We still had the old house. This was a difficulty because we couldn't buy the new house until we sold the one that we were in, especially since the house we wanted to move to was about $80,000 more than the current one. I mean, yes, we now had a steady income, but our last name still wasn't Trump.

Despite all of the stupid mistakes that we continued to make, we had learned some things along the way, so the first thing we did was pray to sell the house. (I told you we had learned some things, aren't you proud of us?) After you are done with your congratulatory nods and approving smiles, I must tell you that after the word "pray" the things that we did right ended and the things that we did wrong began.

Take careful note of the fact that we prayed to sell the house. Remember that at the end of the story, and you will see that we had learned some things, but we still had a long, long way to go. In spite of the fact that we prayed for a specific, "Ben-solution," God still answered and said that He would sell the house. We thought great! Now we don't have to worry. We thought it would be prudent to remind Him about the timeframe that we were dealing with, because for some reason bankers don't like to wait around.

After we "clued Him in" on the razor-sharp timing that He would have to employ on the house sale, we asked Him how much we should sell the house for. He told us a figure that was well over what we bought the house and property for. We hesitated for a moment, but then warmed to the idea. After all, He knows best. When we thought about it, though, the amount seemed about right, because we had completely remodeled and sided the house, which raised the value considerably.

Then, just to be extra holy, I asked Him when I should list it with a realtor. He put it in my heart that He would sell it, and we shouldn't list it. This is where my faith started to journey into uncharted waters. I figured He knew what he was talking about, though, so my mouth said, "OK, we won't list it."

I told Pam that we weren't going to list the house, and that God was going to sell the house. She didn't say anything. She just looked at me with the patient look of someone who has dealt with a mental incompetent before. I did see her looking at my shirt size later that day though, maybe to tell the psych ward what size straight jacket I needed. Actually, she was remarkably calm about the whole idea of not listing the house and so we plunged forward in faith.

A week went by and the house wasn't sold. This was not good news. Ostensibly, we had a month before we needed to make an offer on the new property. One quarter of that time had passed and we hadn't sold the house. We didn't even have an offer. Nobody was interested, or had even come to look at the house. Work out the timeline here: usually it takes anywhere from three weeks to a month to close on a real estate deal. That means we had oh, about NO time left if we were going to meet our self-imposed one-month deadline to start the purchase of the new house. I mean, what was going on?! I was getting antsy.

Then I thought, maybe I could help this process out. I reasoned that the reason that nobody had bought our house yet was that nobody knew about it. (Notice how quickly I started to rely on my own strength to solve the problem instead of trusting God? I told you I still had a long, long way to go.) Anyway, I was following conventional wisdom. I ran an advertising agency, I could design an ad and put it in the newspaper. I said, "God, look, You seem as if you could use some help here, why don't I run an ad in the newspaper and draw in some people." He said: "No."

I was a bit hurt! After all, I was trying to help! I tried plan B. "Well, if I can't run an advertisement, can I at least put it in the classifieds?" He said, "Sure." I breathed a sigh of relief and picked up the phone. But then He went on: "Sure, you can list it in the classifieds if you want to waste your money. I'm going to sell this house."

I was getting a bit frustrated with this situation. How was God going to sell this house if no one knew about it? How was anyone going to know about it without my help? After all, I knew better than God, even if I didn't create the universe in six days! Yes, yes, I have an incredibly over-developed sense of self importance.

After my little bout with overrating my significance though, I decided to trust Him. He said He would do it, so it was His problem, not mine. I don't know if I was waiting for Him to fail so that I could tease Him a little bit, but, for future reference, if you are waiting for God to screw up, so that you can prove yourself right, you will be waiting a long time!

We told everyone we knew that we had a house for sale. That should help, right—telling all ten of our acquaintances that the house was for sale? Nothing was happening! Then, a few days later, we heard of some folks that might be interested. We talked with them, almost salivating over the possibility that they might be the solution to the situation. We told them the price for the house and the full 20 acres. We told them a lesser price for the house and 10 acres. We were nice, we were charming, we were affable. We didn't hear from them again.

Two weeks went by, then three weeks. We were getting desperate. We weren't "crash your car into a telephone pole, collect on the insurance and use it for a down payment" desperate, but that was probably because all of the phone lines in our area were buried. No telephone poles! Seriously, though, we thought maybe we had heard God wrong in this situation and that we had missed the opportunity to list our house.

The fourth week arrived. This was the week we needed to make an offer on the new house. We just weren't sure what to do. We knew the house we wanted in Muskegon would be sold before long if we didn't move on it soon. I was getting ready to do my victory dance because I thought God had failed, but all of the fun had drained out of it, like water through a sieve.

That Sunday, totally dejected, and not at all sure that we heard God correctly, we went to church. We looked over, and there was the woman that had been interested in the house. We asked her where they were on the house issue, but what I really wanted to say was; "Why in the world didn't you get back to us?!" She seemed a little sheepish about the whole issue and said that they had come and looked at the property and loved it, but they just couldn't afford it right now. Then it came to me in a flash of brilliance. "What about a lease with an option to buy?" Her eyes lit up as she considered this possibility.

Look at the way this was working out; because of the rental income that we were going to receive, we would be able to put in a purchase offer on the house in Muskegon. We would also able to obtain bank financing. The leasers would cover all of the electric, gas and upkeep costs. If they purchased at the end of the two-year lease term, then we would have sold our house with minimal muss and fuss, if they didn't, then we were ahead two year's rental income.

Later that week, we met with her and her husband and drew up the papers for a lease with an option to buy. They immediately wrote out a check for the first year's rent and moved in.

I would like to say that after two years, they bought the house and everything worked out according to my well thought-out plan, but that wasn't the case.

One year and nine months came and went. We broached the subject of the purchase option with our leasers, but because of some family issues, they were not going to be able to purchase. They were looking to move out of the area. Oh drat! So much for my perfect plan!

This came at an especially bad time because I had just moved from my job as a pastor (with a steady paycheck) to starting a new ministry dedicated to supporting and encouraging the arts in Christians and churches (without any paycheck, whatsoever.) Not only did I not have enough money to pay what I would be losing in rent, I didn't even have enough money to cover my own house payments. God is working that out, but that is a story for another day. Anyway, needless to say, I was stressed!

I later realized that I really didn't have to be so neurotic. Even before the previous tenants had moved out, I had another person interested in renting the house, two people interested in buying the house, and two different people interested in buying the extra land. I don't know how the whole situation will turn out, but at least now I know that God will indeed sell my house. In fact, I'm kind of excited to see the possibilities pop into view, because my wildest imagination couldn't write a story with this intricate of a plot! His plan may not be in the timing that I think is appropriate, or in the way that I think is best, but when I look back from the other end, I will realize how perfect it was all along.

It's All a Timing Issue

Did you ever notice that God doesn't seem to move on our timing? Ever? The timing that we assign to situations are not even remotely close to when He thinks things should be done! It can get a little alarming!

The Bible states it best: "With the Lord a day is like a thousand years, and a thousand years are like a day." (2 Peter 3:8 NIV) Now, I have yet to wait a thousand years for God to move on my behalf, but sometimes it seems like it. Have you ever felt that way? You are in the midst of "the valley of the shadow of death" and are looking around wondering where the vaulted salvation is that you have read so much about. God says that He will save you in the time of trouble. Proverbs 11: 8 says "The righteous man is rescued from trouble…" (NIV) So where is the help?

Then at the eleventh hour, God comes in and solves the situation, usually in a way that is much different that any scenario that you could have come up with! Admit it, you've been there! Why does it seem like God waits until all hope is gone before He acts? It's all a question of timing.

God has never been late in fulfilling His promises, but it sure seems like He has missed an awful lot of opportunities to be early. Take the story of Lazarus found in John 11 for example. Lazarus, the brother of Mary and Martha was sick. They sent word to Jesus to come and heal him. Jesus made a promise that Lazarus' sickness wouldn't end in death. Then he sat around for two more days.

By the time Jesus finally got to Mary, Martha and Lazarus' hometown, Lazarus had been dead and buried for four days. Hmmm. At this point I would have been doubting Jesus' promise that Lazarus' sickness wouldn't end in death!

At any rate, Jesus plunged ahead and told them to move the big rock that covered the cave where Lazarus lay dead. They looked at him with disbelief oozing out of their eyes and said in essence, "What, are you nuts? He's been in there long enough that he stinks!" Jesus told them to do it anyway.

So they removed the rock, Jesus told Lazarus to come out, and in a few moments, a mummy came hopping out of the tomb. Lazarus was alive!

My question is this: why did Jesus wait two extra days before He went to heal Lazarus? It was a matter of timing. You see, the Jews of that time believed that for up to three days a person's spirit hung around their body when they died and so if Jesus would have raised him right away, it would have been easier to write off as a "natural" occurrence. That could be one reason. Or it could have been important to have that amount of time in order to build Mary and Martha's faith. Or it may be any number of reasons we haven't even thought of. The important thing to remember is that God's timing is perfect, but it hardly ever matches up with ours.

The point is this: God knows and takes into account every single important factor when He moves on your behalf. He knows what the stock market will do, He knows what it will take to build your faith, He even knows what the weather will be like. He takes all of those factors into consideration and works out the plan and timing that is going to benefit you the most.

That's why we have to trust Him. Just like a father has a better idea what is best for his child because he has more experience, God knows what's best for us because of his vastly superior experience. He knows the exact time when things will work. He knows how all the pieces fit together. "The Lord is not slow in keeping His promise, as some understand slowness." (2 Peter 3:9 NIV)

Take a look at the story of the sale of our house. Our plan would have been to list with a real estate agent, put the house on the market and hopefully sell in a short amount of time. If we would have followed that plan, so many things could have gone wrong, not the least of which we probably wouldn't have sold the house in a timely fashion.

Now look at the timing of the plan that God put together. We had renters for the house in just under a month. By the time we had those renters, the house we wanted to buy had been on the market for three months and the sellers were very anxious to sell, so they were more amenable to our offer. They had also dropped the price by ten thousand dollars. We will be able to sell our house at our convenience. We had lessees that would take care of the house, and at the end of two years could decide to buy the house or not. If they didn't buy, we just made two years worth of rent on top of the amount of the sale. Plus, we would have paid down the amount we owed on the house by another two years. It was a no-lose situation. And we didn't have to pay the real estate agent fee of eight percent.

The way that God is working out the situation is nothing we could have thought of—it's too intricate, dependent on so many fragile things to fit together. But it will put extra money in our pocket, it has increased our faith, and showed us the greatness of our God. It was all about His plan and His timing. We could never have orchestrated it so perfectly.

In the past I thought knowing God's plan was the pinnacle of being in God's will, but through many experiences like this, I have come to realize that just as important as knowing God's will, you must know His timing.

What would have happened if Noah had waited for 50 years before starting to build the ark? Or what if Moses had tried to lead Israel through the Red Sea before God parted it? What would have happened if Jesus would have decided to take a vacation to Damascus when he was supposed to be in Gethsemane before His arrest, trial, and crucifixion? What would have happened if Jesus just didn't rise on the third day?

Not only is God faithful in His plan for your life, He is faithful in His timing of that plan. God will always show up. When you call on Him, He WILL rescue you! Don't fret if "Lazarus" has been in the grave four days, just know that Jesus is on His way. And instead of forging ahead or lagging behind, trust in His plan and His timing.

Missions, Money and the Callings of God

Twentyfour teenagers, ninety-eight degree heat, two vans, one where the air conditioner blew out hot air, a trailer and a fourteen hour drive. What could be more fun? Maybe an appendectomy. Or oral surgery.

The youth group from our church was going on a missions trip. Hey now! (I'm reprimanding those of you that said "Good riddance" when you read that last sentence.) In any case, most missions trips go to exotic foreign countries and minister to indigenous people groups. Our youth group, on the other hand, was going to Boonsville, Arkansas. So much for exotic.

When I heard about the trip, my first thought was—"I want to go on a missions trip." My second thought was—"I don't want to go on THIS missions trip." I mean nothing against teens or Arkansas, but "Come on!" I had been on a missions trip before to Guatemala and it had been a life-changing experience. My spiritual life was in need of a boost. A missions trip would be the perfect way to allow God the chance to get my attention. But in my mind, this trip wasn't for me.

I didn't think any more about it. I just kept my eyes open for an opportunity to be part of God's plan (as long as it wasn't to Arkansas.) I don't know what it was about the missions trip to Arkansas that put it in the category of things I didn't want to do, maybe it was the location, the timing, the teenagers, you take your pick. God has such a sense of humor, though, doesn't He?

Anyway, it was about two weeks until the youth group was scheduled to leave on their trip. I was still blissfully in my state of looking for the "perfect" missions opportunity and I had to see the youth pastor about something. As we were talking, I asked how things were going for the missions trip. He said that one of the kids had dropped out and he was trying to fill their space. Then he looked at me with a knowing smirk on his face and said: "YOU should take their place."

In that moment, God's "sinister" plan was unveiled before my very eyes! He was going to make me go on this missions trip! I was going to have to be a babysitter for 24 teenagers! I was frightened. I was exasperated! I was appalled! I was interested. I began to seriously consider the possibility of going and the thought came into my mind. "I SHOULD go on this missions trip." Suddenly, I wanted to go! THIS was the opportunity that God had for me. I didn't have to wait for an overseas mission to the Ukraine or learn a different language to minister to the pygmies in Africa, God wanted to use me on this trip. I was just too dumb to see it!

It had taken me a good twenty minutes to work through my angst, so after I made the decision to go, I called the youth pastor and told him. He went on to explain that the person who had vacated the position had about $200 in their account that he would apply that amount to my trip. The total cost of the trip was $430, so I only had to come up with $230. I was elated.

There was one problem. I didn't have $230. We had come up against some emergencies and our accounts were drained. We had over $2,500 in unexpected expenses in one month! Thankfully, the youth pastor said that I didn't have come up with the funds right away, because of the late notice etcetera. In spite of his generous offer, I still wanted to get the money in on time. Unfortunately, that didn't change the fact that I didn't have it.

I thought our financial situation would get better and I could take the money from our checking account, I mean it was only $230, right? But of course, our finances got worse. I guess I should have known that might happen, it takes a while to recover from a major financial blow. Meanwhile, the youth pastor came to me and said that he wanted to split the money that I was going to get toward the trip with another leader. So instead of owing $230, I suddenly owe $330. This situation just kept getting better and better, huh?

I am happy to say that I still wasn't stressed about the money that we didn't have for the missions trip that I hadn't wanted to go on, but my wife was. Oh she of little faith! Ah, who am I kidding, I'm no paragon of trust most of the time either! Actually, she was the catalyst for the way this story turns out.

It was down to the last Thursday before we were to leave on the trip. All the money was supposed to be in that day. I, of course, had submitted zero. My wife had reached maximum stress, unbeknownst to me. I might have kind of, sort of neglected to tell her that we didn't have to have the money in right away. Hey, stop looking at me that way, it's not like you never made a mistake! In any event, she went to work and on the way, she saved our bacon. She prayed. She asked God to provide the money for my trip.

I'm not quite sure why I didn't pray for God to provide the money other than the recurring fact that I try to do everything by myself and it's only when I fall flat on my heinie, that I ask God for help. Annoying personality trait to have, huh? Thankfully, Pam kept me from having to go through that.

I was standing in the church office talking with the mother of one of the teenagers that was going on the trip. We were talking about very grave and important things like the weather and what food we each were going to have for dinner. All of a sudden she asked me, "Do you owe any more on your trip?" I told her, yes, I did owe money. She asked me "How much?" "$330," I told her. She asked me, "Would $200 help?" I was thinking: "God bless you, you wonderful woman of God, when the petition comes to me nominating you for sainthood, I will be the first to sign it." I said: "Yes! That would be great!"

I only owed $130 on my trip now! We could swing that in the next couple of weeks! I was so excited! I called up my mom to tell her about the cool thing that God had just done paying for part of my missions trip. She was very enthused as well. We talked about a bunch of stuff, mainly how the rest of the family was doing and what the latest news on the home front was. I never asked for any money from her. We had a great time visiting, and were getting ready to hang up when she said, "I want to cover the rest of your trip."

I was flabbergasted. It wasn't that my mother wasn't a generous person, because she is, it was just the way in which God orchestrated the entire situation. He didn't leave any little bit out, even to the fact that my entire trip was paid for before I went—without sending out any support letters or anything. I never had to worry about the money coming in, when it was needed, it was just there.

We went on the trip and for me it was a life-changing experience! God used the time to confirm some things that He had been speaking into my life. He solidified the calling He had placed on me and overall, just made me feel incredibly loved and valued in His eyes.

We did service projects for some of the people in the area. It was 118 degrees and we worked in the sun all day long, but it was such a blessing to us! As we painted, fixed windows, and got to know these people, we were amazed at their lives and their genuine love for God. I came away shamed at the shallowness of my affection for God. I mean here were people who had so very little, but their love for God ran so deep, I felt like a hypocrite! While I stood there with so much given to me and a love for God that seemed so thin, it barely covered the naked greed that ran in my bones.

Maybe it was realizations like these, or maybe it was something else entirely, but for whatever reason, I came away from that missions trip a different man. Not perfect, but changed. Realizing and accepting the purpose of my life, whatever that is.

This was not the trip I would have chosen to go on. Once I was on the trip, things were definitely not the way I expected—I had expected to see abject poverty, but we just came across people that were a little less fortunate than us. But it didn't matter what I expected or what I had chosen, this was the path that God had chosen for me, because He knew what I needed, not what I wanted. Mostly, He knew what it would take to reach my heart.

The Provision of God's Plan

A great percentage of Christians never realize their potential in God, because they aren't willing to do what it takes to follow His plan. They are scared of the abyss of the unknown, unwilling to jump into the place where they are so far removed from control of their lives that to attempt to regain it would send them into a tailspin. They are comfortable in slow mediocrity. I don't blame them. There are areas in my life where I can't let go. There are places of faith that I am still unwilling to go—I'm scared to trembling of the consequences. But I am trying. I desire with more of a longing than I have for air to join the elite that have made the arduous journey and stand on the ragged edge of faith.

You see, I have tasted just a small portion of what that type of life is like. I have stood in mouth-open awe at the way God's plan has come together. I have seen His hands rescue me at the peak of my stupidity, and He has loved me like no one can.

Yes, God's plan is well worth following, and the thing I have learned is that when you follow His plan with all of your heart, His provision is there. His plan and His provision go hand-in-hand. When He makes known the plan, He has already worked out the way that He is going to provide everything you need to do it. You don't need to "go and buy AA batteries" to make it work! (And all of you with small children, together now; "Yea!")

Take this story for example. God's plan was for me to go on this trip. It took me a bit of time to get His will through my big, thick skull, but once I did, I jumped in wholeheartedly. Or foolhardily, take your choice.

I had no idea where the money was going to come from, in fact I never even gave the money a thought, I just knew that this was God's will.

Because of my faith in following His plan, He took care of all of my needs. Even those I didn't know that I would have. For example, I didn't know that I was going to need Him to miraculously provide the money for the trip, I thought I could cover that. Fortunately, He knew and He had a plan for it well in advance.

Often times in the past, I have spent way too long looking at the circumstances. Sometimes I still do that. The only thing I really should be concerned with is: "What is God's will in this situation? What does He want me to do?" If I find that, and I follow that no matter what circumstances surround me, He will take care of the rest.

Don't approach things the way I do a lot of times. I know what God wants me to do, but then I run down a list of the reasons that it won't work, or I shouldn't do it, or ways that it could fail. When God tells you make a leap, take a step, jump or hop, just do it. He will work out the details. Job 42:2 says, "I'm convinced: You can do anything and everything. Nothing and no one can upset Your plans." (MSG)

In this missions trip, God brought in the money that I needed in a way that I couldn't take credit for. He provided for me to go because it was His plan for me to go.

This lesson has served me well as God took the next step and called me to start a new ministry. All of the circumstances around me told me that I should continue doing what I was doing—I had a steady paycheck, the ministries I was in charge of were flourishing—in fact, they almost ran themselves! Things were going well. Unfortunately, God kept tugging at my heart to start this new ministry. I knew this was God's plan.

Because I learned about His provision, when I was sure starting a ministry was the calling that He had for me, I stepped forward. I (willingly, this time) went from a steady job and paycheck to a difficult job with no paycheck.

The strange thing was that there was peace about the decision. I knew that I had made the right decision. I won't say there wasn't worry as Pam and I sat down to the monumental task of trimming $4,000 a month from our budget, but the stress and the worry seemed insignificant in the overwhelming brightness of the peace of knowing that we were going to be taken care of. We knew God would provide.

Don't be afraid to follow the plans that God has for you, He will meet your needs when you follow Him. Look at Matthew 6:25-34, I know we've all heard it before, but it bears repeating. "If you decide for God, living a life of God-worship, it follows that you don't fuss about what's on the table at mealtimes or whether the clothes in your closet are in fashion. There is far more to your life than the food you put in your stomach, more to your outer appearance than the clothes you hang on your body. Look at the birds, free and unfettered, not tied down to a job description, careless in the care of God and you count far more to Him than birds. Has anyone by fussing in front of the mirror ever gotten taller by so much as an inch? All this time and money wasted on fashion—do you think it makes that much difference? Instead of looking at the fashions, walk out into the fields and look at the wildflowers. They never primp or shop, but have you ever seen color and design quite like it? The ten best-dressed men and women in the country look shabby alongside them. If God gives such attention to the appearance of wildflowers—most of which are never even seen—don't you think He'll attend to you, take pride in you, do His best for you? What I'm trying to do here is to get you to relax, to not be so preoccupied with getting, so you can respond to God's giving. People who don't know God and the way He works fuss over these things, but you know both God and how He works. Steep your life in God-reality, God-initiative, God-provisions. Don't worry about missing out. You'll find all your everyday human concerns will be met. Give your entire attention to what God is doing right now, and don't get worked up about what may or may not happen tomorrow. God will help you deal with whatever hard things come up when the time comes." (MSG)

The big thing to keep in mind is that when God puts together a plan, He has made it a package deal. It's like going to the travel agent to book an all-inclusive vacation. They find you the correct flight, they have a limo waiting at the airport to pick you up. Your hotel has a reservation booked by your agent. Your tour guide shows up at the proper time. Your meals are taken care of. All you have to do is get on the plane. In the same way, when God calls you to something, He has the plan all marked out. There are no unexpected costs, side trips or problems. You don't even have to look for the fine print, there are no additional costs. He has paid for the whole thing because He is not only the "travel agent" but He is also the "financier." All we have to do is follow His itinerary.

I know, I know it sounds really easy, but it's a bit harder to actually walk it out. But if you boil this truth down to its essence, that's all there is to it—God has a plan for you, and if you follow His plan, He will also provide everything you need to complete His plan. Simple, huh? So pray for the courage to take those steps of faith, and pray for the faith to believe in His provision.

Write your own story

This book is the product of several years engaging in the practice of keeping a log of God's faithfulness. Whenever something significant would happen to me, I would write it down. I would tell the truth about the situation, I wouldn't try to slant it one way or another. Sometimes I would even put down my ideas about how the situation would work out. Later, when something would happen to amend the story, I would go back and put that in as well.

During times of great stress, humiliation, or difficulty, I would go back and read my "God's Faithfulness Log." Reliving those instances helped me to believe for greatness from God in my current situation. Seeing how He was faithful in my life in the past, helped me to trust in His faithfulness for the future.

Even more than that, I began to see some patterns in the way that God worked. I saw that no matter what, God was faithful. I saw how He always dealt with me in love (a difficult task sometimes, trust me!) I saw how in every single instance the way God worked in the here and now proved true His Bible promises—promises like "I will take care of you," and "I will protect you," and even "I will hold you when you cry."

The stories began to speak to me. They taught me about some of God's attributes. They helped me to learn from my mistakes. Looking at how God dealt with me in different situations in my life really helped me to see Him more clearly.

I would encourage you to start your own "God's Faithfulness Log." It doesn't have to be a book. It doesn't have to use correct grammar or even make sense to anyone but you. It is for you. It will help you to remind yourself when times are tough to keep going. It will remind you that God is not dead, that as recently as last week He may have done something amazing in your life. And as you see God's loving care of you throughout your life, you will love Him all the more.

I have had people come to me and say that my faith has inspired them. Trust me, I don't feel very inspiring most of the time. Please don't get the idea that I walk several feet off the ground because I'm so holy or so close to God. I am like you.

Most of my decisions to follow Him are not confident declarations of faith, followed by assured steps forward. Most are terror-filled, small steps, questioning, doubtful, quailing, and scared.

I still ask Him if He knows what He is doing. I still take over the driver's seat, relinquishing only when it is abundantly clear that I have driven us into a ditch. I am a normal person. I have all of your fears, doubts and foibles.

I am white-knuckled in my reluctance to leave my comfortable existence and walk the hard road of faith. Don't think that there is something fundamentally different in my physiological makeup that cries out for the unknown, shifting sand of faith. There's not. If I had it my way, I would stay on the safe, comfortable couch forever.

The problem is that I have tasted faith. I know what it is like to see God come through against impossible odds. I know that He calls us to more than we can do on our own. I have read the stories of others who have trusted Him and seen the things that were accomplished through their lives. I have pondered all of these things and I have determined that I want that for myself.

I want my life to mean something. I want to see what God can do with a life, even one as insignificant as mine, that is devoted to Him. I want it so bad that nothing will hold me back from straining after Him—nothing will stand in the way.

God is faithful. Unfortunately, it's not something that can be learned vicariously. For it to truly sink deep enough into your core to make a difference, it has to be experienced. Just like a small child learns to trust their parents to be there for him, so we, through time and experience, learn to trust that God will be there for us.

God is faithful. There is nothing that you can do to make Him more or less faithful, He always is and always has been. It is His nature. You can trust in His faithfulness.

Let the net of His faithfulness be your failsafe as His plan calls you to do things that seem foolhardy. Throw caution to the wind and abandon yourself to the freedom of His plan. You won't regret it.

It is not an easy road, the road of faithfulness, but it is worth it. And at the end of your life as you stand at the summit of the sheer, treacherous mountain that the faithfulness of God helped you climb, as the frigid air stings your eyes, you will know pride. You will have lived. You will have thrown off the blanket of mediocrity and walked the hard road. And because you dared to trust His faithfulness, you will have accomplished something for eternity—something that won't be burned off like the chaff of earning money for yourself or trying to claw your way to the top of the corporate ladder. You will have made a difference in the world.

And as you stand there, you will breathe so deep of the cold, crisp air and you will know that you wouldn't have had it any other way. You won't regret a single step of the journey. The only things that you will regret are those steps you didn't take—the times you held back, trembling, unable or unwilling to make the jump that faith required.

As the light of your life burns down to brilliant red as the sun sets, you will hear a voice—a voice that thrills and terrifies you at the same time. The voice's power will make your body shudder with low frequency vibrations as your heart quickens with anticipation as you wait for the one you have longed for, for so long.

A warmth like you have never known will enfold you in its arms. The cold doesn't bother you anymore. An urgency and peace coexist inexplicably with each other in your bosom as you strain to hear the voice. And then the voice speaks.

With the mingled sounds of a raging river and a child's laughter God says those words you have waited so long to hear; "Well done my good and faithful friend. Welcome home."